FIX-IT GUIDE FOR WOMEN

Dorothy Carbo

Published 1976 by Arco Publishing Company, Inc.
219 Park Avenue South, New York, N.Y. 10003
by arrangement with Fawcett Publications, Inc.

Copyright © 1975 by Fawcett Publications, Inc.

Printed in the United States of America

Library of Congress Cataloging in Publication Data

Carbo, Dorothy.
  Fix-it guide for women.

  Originally published by Fawcett Publications,
Greenwich, Connecticut.
  1. Repairing—Amateurs manuals. I. Title
TT151.C28 1976   643'.7   76-21255
ISBN 0-668-04016-5 pbk.

ARCO PUBLISHING COMPANY INC.
219 Park Avenue South, New York, N.Y. 10003

Fix-It Guide For Women

Table of Contents

Introduction

Very often a woman is at home alone when some household device breaks down. She then has several alternatives. . . .

She can call the nearest male, but one is not usually available.

She can throw it away or do without it, but this will soon lead her to either the poor house or the inconvenience of cave life.

She can sit down and cry, although this option will leave her with one wet hanky and one still-broken object.

Or, she can fix it! Here's the perfect choice. Not only does she discover how capable she is, but she saves lots of money that might otherwise go to repairmen. The bonuses are a safer, smoother-running home, and a great feeling of accomplishment, creativity, enjoyment and involvement.

Don't be mystified! There is no mystique about home repair and tools that a little basic information won't dissolve. My only head start is that I have had the opportunity to handle and use tools from early youth—just as every professional repairman learned what he knows. There is no need for special talent or a unique kind of intelligence. If you can read and have normal functioning of both hands, you can fix. There is nothing in this book that you cannot do. The simple step-by-step instructions have been tested by women who had never held a wrench in their lives—so success is assured.

You can take a giant step toward feeling at ease by taking a trip to your local hardware store, lumber yard or home improvement center. Browse around. Familiarize yourself with the tools and supplies available. Compare products and prices. Ask questions. Chat with the salesmen and customers. This will come to be a place you enjoy visiting. (Expect to be called "lady" when they get used to having you around.)

Then all it takes is for you to try—you'll probably amaze yourself and others.

Happy fixing!

The Basic Tool Kit

What you need and how to use it.

Historically, it was when man first learned to make and use tools that he began to shape his destiny and control his environment. And so shall it be with *women!*

Here are the tools you need for a basic tool kit, and a brief idea of what each is used for. Treat yourself to quality tools whenever possible—they last longer and work better.

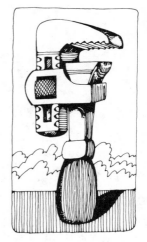

Monkey Wrench: *Has an adjustable head for large bolts or pipe joints. It comes in many sizes, and is vital for plumbing repair work.*

Flat Wrench: *Also called an open-ended wrench, it comes with different size openings at each end and is sold in sets. Used for turning nuts and bolts.*

Adjustable Wrench: *The head can adjust to various sizes to fit the job. The tool itself comes in a few sizes.*

Combination Pliers: *Use this for holding or bending, but do not use it on nuts unless a wrench is not available, since that tends to damage the face of the nut. The slip-joint allows the jaws to open at the hinge for gripping larger objects (very handy for opening stubborn bottle-tops).*

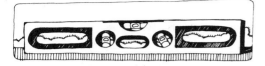

Spirit Level: *This comes in many sizes, and is used to check whether the work is parallel or perpendicular to the ground. Place level on or against edge being checked. A small float ball or air bubble indicates center or direction of lean for correction. A vital tool for shelf hanging, door installation or repair, and appliance functioning.*

Plane: *Shaves off excess wood, to trim and smooth surfaces. Use for trimming a sticking door.*

Combination Square: *A device combining a ruler, a square (to insure accurate 90° cuts), a level, and a 45° line. There's also a gauge for edge marking.*

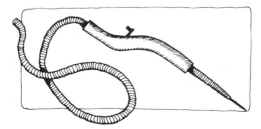

Snake (Auger): *When drains don't respond to plunger action, this is used to clear out something lodged in a turn in the plumbing. The cable is cranked through the pipes until it reaches the obstruction.*

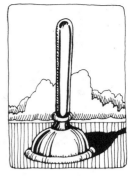

Plunger: *Used to clear drains by use of suction and air pressure. Place firmly over the drain and press down—the suction formed will dislodge any objects or clogs. A newly marketed item called an* air plunger *uses the same principles with a small handle and concentrated air pressure.*

Claw Hammer: *An all-purpose, very important tool used for driving nails. The back part can be used for prying. The center slot is used for removing nails (just slip the slot under the edges of the nail and rock the hammer to lift the nail up).*

Mallet: *For pounding when a heavier hammer might leave damaging marks, such as on leather or soft wood. It can also be used for pounding to loosen heavy pipe joints, or on a metal chisel.*

Hack Saw: *Cuts metals, pipes and cables. The blades are changeable for different metals.*

Sabre Saw: *A lightweight almost indispensable tool for any cutting job. The blades are changeable for different grades of wood, metal, plastic. Don't shy away from small power tools—if you can handle an electric kitchen knife, you can handle a sabre saw. It is, in fact, much easier and faster than a hand saw, and not that much more expensive.*

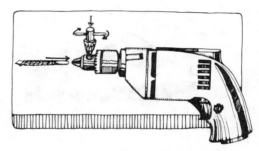

Electric Drill: *A lightweight, almost indispensable tool for all hole making purposes. Attachments are available for sawing, sanding, polishing, grinding and more. It comes in several larger sizes, but ¼-inch is fine for most household jobs. The key is used to open and firmly close the chucks or jaws that hold the drilling bit.*

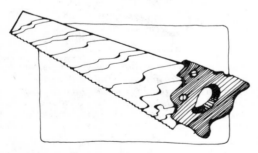

Hand Saw: *There are various sizes of these. Teeth spacing and set determine whether it is a crosscut saw (meant to cut across the grain) or a rip saw (for cutting with the grain of the wood).*

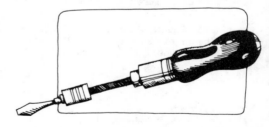

Ratchet: *This drill has a push-pull action. It takes several size drill bits and screwdriver heads. A most handy tool if the electric drill is not your choice. Also called a Yankeeman drill.*

The Basic Tool Kit

Crank-type Hand Drill: *Has the same uses as the ratchet, but has a crank action like an egg-beater.*

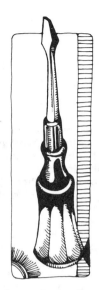

Screwdriver: *Comes in a variety of lengths and thickness, so start out with a thin one and a wide one. Use with screws that have straight slots cut in the head.*

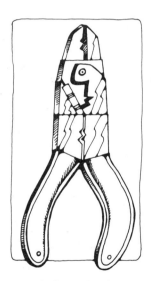

Wire Stripper: *To remove the insulation from wire, and to cut wire. Can neatly strip a wire without cutting into the metal.*

Phillips Screwdriver: *Has a four-pronged pointed tip for use with screws that have cross-cut heads.*

Here are a few basics about nails, screws, nuts, bolts and special fasteners:

Nails with flat heads on them are called common nails; those without heads are called finishing nails. When strong fastening is required, common nails are used. When the nail is to be set slightly below the surface and hidden, finishing nails are used and *countersunk* (tapped with a pointed metal tool to drive it below the surface).

Special nails include ornamental upholstery nails, staple or U-nails for holding wire in place, corrugated nails for joining two pieces of wood on the same plane (as in a picture frame), and concrete nails.

Screws have a spiral threading that starts at a point, allowing penetration into wood or wall surface. The heads are slotted to receive a screwdriver, or cross-slotted to receive a phillips head screwdriver. Heads of screws can be flat, round or oval. The round head meets the surface flush. For the flat or oval head, the wood or metal needs to be countersunk (shaped to accept the slant of the screw).

Bolts are like flat-bottomed screws.

They do not penetrate material, but must be secured with nuts. Their heads can be slotted, to be turned with a screwdriver, or squared or hexagonal, to be turned with a wrench.

Nuts are the threaded pieces which turn onto bolts and secure them in place. They come squared, hexagonal, wing-shaped for hand turning, and capped for a finished effect.

Special fasteners are needed for installation into brick, masonry, plaster or hollow walls. Instructions for each situation appear later in the book.

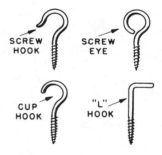

SCREW HOOK

SCREW EYE

CUP HOOK

"L" HOOK

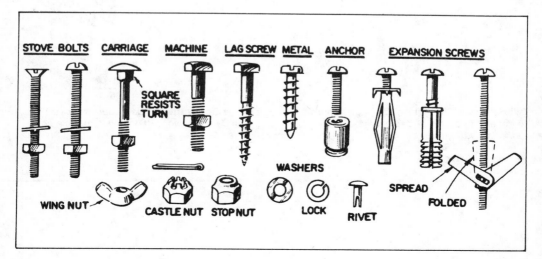

STOVE BOLTS CARRIAGE MACHINE LAG SCREW METAL ANCHOR EXPANSION SCREWS

SQUARE RESISTS TURN

WING NUT CASTLE NUT STOP NUT WASHERS LOCK RIVET SPREAD FOLDED

The Basic Tool Kit

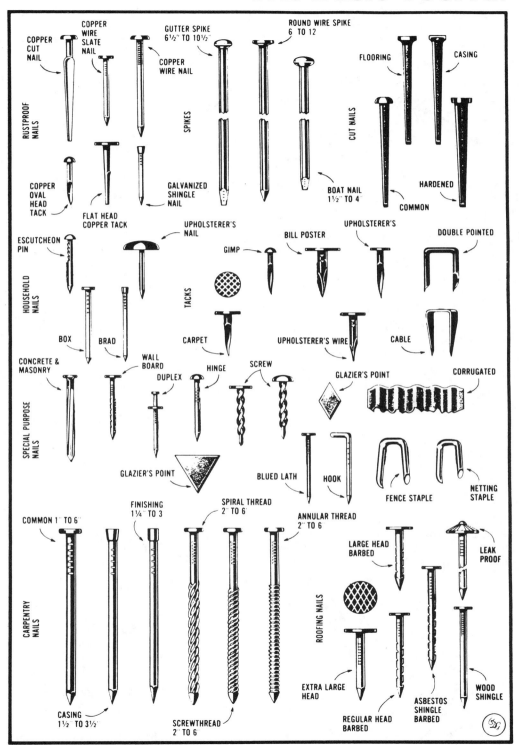

RUSTPROOF NAILS

COPPER CUT NAIL

COPPER WIRE SLATE NAIL

COPPER WIRE NAIL

GUTTER SPIKE 6½" TO 10½"

ROUND WIRE SPIKE 6 TO 12

SPIKES

FLOORING

CASING

CUT NAILS

COPPER OVAL HEAD TACK

FLAT HEAD COPPER TACK

GALVANIZED SHINGLE NAIL

BOAT NAIL 1½" TO 4"

HARDENED

COMMON

HOUSEHOLD NAILS

ESCUTCHEON PIN

UPHOLSTERER'S NAIL

GIMP

BILL POSTER

UPHOLSTERER'S

DOUBLE POINTED

TACKS

BOX

BRAD

CARPET

UPHOLSTERER'S WIRE

CABLE

SPECIAL PURPOSE NAILS

CONCRETE & MASONRY

WALL BOARD

DUPLEX

HINGE

SCREW

GLAZIER'S POINT

CORRUGATED

GLAZIER'S POINT

BLUED LATH

HOOK

FENCE STAPLE

NETTING STAPLE

CARPENTRY NAILS

COMMON 1" TO 6"

FINISHING 1¼" TO 3

SPIRAL THREAD 2" TO 6"

ANNULAR THREAD 2" TO 6

CASING 1½" TO 3½"

SCREWTHREAD 2" TO 6"

ROOFING NAILS

LARGE HEAD BARBED

LEAK PROOF

EXTRA LARGE HEAD

REGULAR HEAD BARBED

ASBESTOS SHINGLE BARBED

WOOD SHINGLE

A FEW STAGGERED NAILS (A)
ARE BETTER THAN MANY
IN A LINE (B).

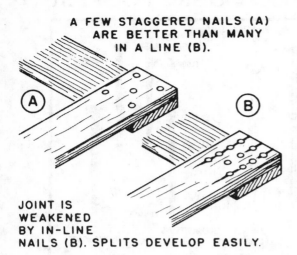

JOINT IS
WEAKENED
BY IN-LINE
NAILS (B). SPLITS DEVELOP EASILY.

NAILS CLINCHED WITH THE
GRAIN ARE WEAKER.....

...THAN NAILS
CLINCHED
ACROSS
THE GRAIN

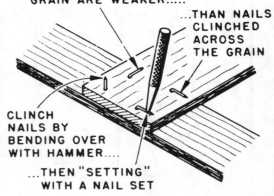

CLINCH
NAILS BY
BENDING OVER
WITH HAMMER....

...THEN "SETTING"
WITH A NAIL SET

CONCEAL NAILHEAD BY LIFTING
CHIP--- THEN GLUING DOWN AGAIN
AFTER NAIL IS DRIVEN IN.

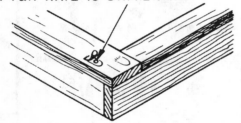

V-NAILING ON EDGES AND ENDS
GIVES MORE STRENGTH.

NAIL SHOULD BE THREE TIMES
THICKNESS OF PIECE BEING NAILED

FLAT-FACED PUNCH CAN
BE USED TO SET FLAT-
HEAD NAILS UNDER
WOOD SURFACE.

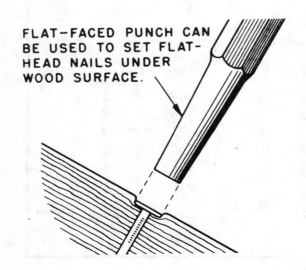

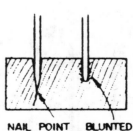

NAIL POINT   BLUNTED
CAN SPLIT   POINT
HARD WOODS   BREAKS
                FIBERS

USE NAIL SET FOR FLUSH JOB

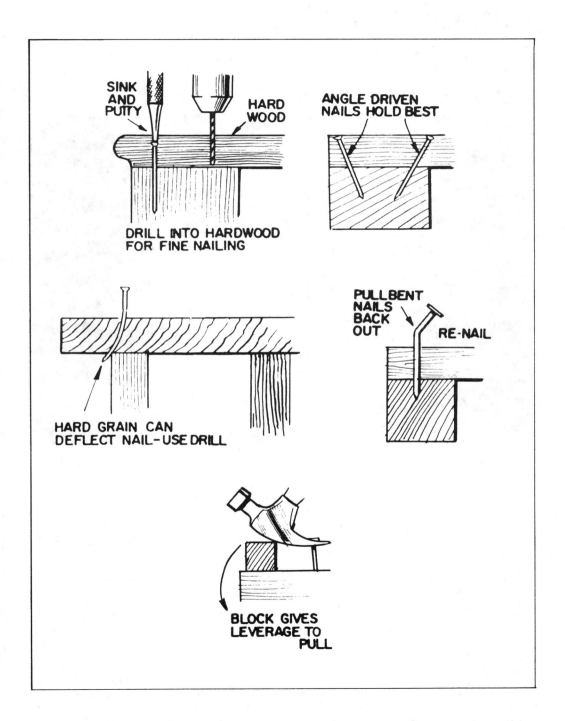

SINK AND PUTTY

HARD WOOD

DRILL INTO HARDWOOD FOR FINE NAILING

ANGLE DRIVEN NAILS HOLD BEST

HARD GRAIN CAN DEFLECT NAIL – USE DRILL

PULL BENT NAILS BACK OUT

RE-NAIL

BLOCK GIVES LEVERAGE TO PULL

Electricity and Current Events

The ABC's of safe electrical work.

A day doesn't go by when you don't use electrical current. Learn how to use it right!

Electricity is awesome, but it isn't magic. If you understand its basics, you'll be able to handle electrical repairs safely and confidently—but always remember the rules and take the simple precautions.

The main source of electricity for your home is your local electric company. It enters your home through wires and passes through meters which determine how much you use, and therefore, how much you should be billed.

In your home, electricity can be shut off at a number of places (switches). The main switch is located at the fuse or circuit box, and it can shut off power for the entire house or apartment. There are also individual switches which control power to individual outlets, plugs or fixtures. Electricity is constantly available at any plugs that are not controlled by switches, so that the switch is in the appliance itself.

Electricity must complete a circular path called a circuit. If there is a break in this path, like an open switch or a burned-out bulb, current will not flow through.

To convert electrical energy to light, heat or mechanical energy, the electrical path must meet with resistance. A short circuit, or "short" occurs if there is no resistance and the electricity flows directly from the electrical source to the ground wire. This blows a fuse; it's too much energy flooding through at one time.

THIS READING IS 66,482 KILOWATT-HOURS

THIS READING IS 66,649 KILOWATT-HOURS

TOTAL BETWEEN TWO IS 167 KILOWATT-HOURS
WHICH IS QUANTITY UTILITY CO. BILLS YOU FOR

Meter is located on outer wall of building.

Shut off main switch in circuit breaker box.

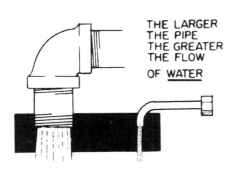

THE LARGER
THE PIPE
THE GREATER
THE FLOW

OF <u>WATER</u>

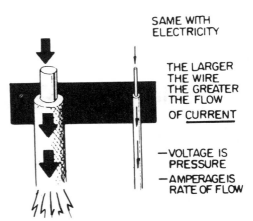

SAME WITH
ELECTRICITY

THE LARGER
THE WIRE
THE GREATER
THE FLOW

OF <u>CURRENT</u>

—VOLTAGE IS
 PRESSURE
—AMPERAGE IS
 RATE OF FLOW

All you need to know about fuses and circuit breakers: The fuse box or circuit breaker box is located next to or along the main switch in your basement, or on an outside wall of the house. In an apartment it can be almost anywhere, and is covered by a small metal door. Find it and become familiar with it.

A fuse box and a circuit breaker both automatically blow out or flip off when too much current is being drawn. This results in all current being shut off to the effected line, therefore stopping the build-up of heat and protecting you from the danger of fire. With a circuit breaker, just flip it back to the "on" position.

You can tell when a fuse is blown by a blackening and a melting and breaking of the metal strip visible through the glass. It unscrews just like a light bulb, and you should keep a supply on hand that are of the *right amperage*. Never use 20 or 30 amp fuses if 15 amps are called for in your circuit.

Cartridge fuses may have pop-out controls.

WATTAGE REQUIREMENTS OF TYPICAL APPLIANCES

Appliance	Wattage	Appliance	Wattage
standard refrigerator	205	iron	1000
dishwasher	1155	sun lamp	390
clothes washer	1000	toaster	990
broiler	1325	waffle maker	855
coffee maker elect.	830	television, black & white	280
floor polisher	240	room air conditioner	800
hair dryer	235	food waste disposal	330
room heater	1095	oil burner	245

Electricity and Current Events

Before replacing a blown fuse, disconnect the appliances on that circuit. Then screw in the new fuse. If it doesn't blow immediately, but blows when you reconnect the appliances, you know you've got an overload on that circuit. Each 15 amp circuit allows 1750 watts of usage, so by checking our wattage chart you may be able to pick out the culprit appliance. Shut off some appliances as a temporary measure to help balance your electricity account. Eventually you may want to install additional wiring.

If the fuse blows immediately, with no appliances plugged in, you may have a short in the line. This often occurs at the ceiling fixture, where wires might get twisted and broken from the movement of the lamp, or damaged by heat if the bulb is too large for the capacity of the fixture. It will require re-wiring, and more care the next time you buy bulbs.

Remove the blown fuse and screw in new one of same amperage.

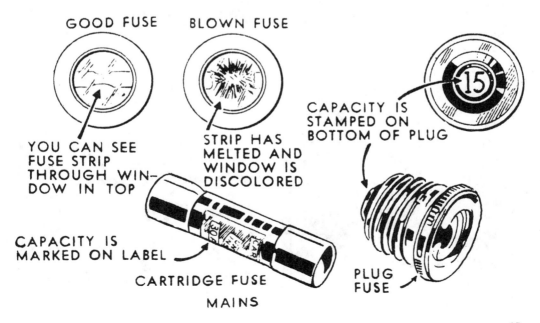

GOOD FUSE

BLOWN FUSE

YOU CAN SEE FUSE STRIP THROUGH WINDOW IN TOP

STRIP HAS MELTED AND WINDOW IS DISCOLORED

CAPACITY IS STAMPED ON BOTTOM OF PLUG

CAPACITY IS MARKED ON LABEL

CARTRIDGE FUSE

MAINS

PLUG FUSE

Safety Tips: Before going any further, you've got to learn the dos and don'ts of electricity.

First and foremost, be sure to throw circuit switch or fuse before attempting any electrical wiring repairs.

Never touch electrical appliances, wiring, or fuses when you're wet or on wet ground.

Always unplug appliances before working on them.

Keep proper size fuses in the fuse box, and never replace blown fuses with larger ones.

Repair or replace any frayed appliance cords or loose plugs.

Follow instructions on all lamps and ceiling fixtures. Don't use larger wattage bulbs than those specified.

Only buy electrical appliances that have been approved by a reliable testing company.

Be sure lamp bulbs have adequate ventilation. Never allow them to come in direct contact with curtains, rugs, paper or cloth items.

Avoid use of multiple outlet plugs on a regular basis, since they increase the chance of an overload.

Never have extension wires running under rug where traffic might cause fraying. This is a great fire hazard.

Be sure all appliances have proper grounding.

Put cap plugs into outlets that children can reach.

Be certain that all sockets and switches have face plate covers.

Always unplug appliance before repairing

Always pull head of plug; don't pull wire.

Break the circuit before doing major work.

Don't overload circuit with multiple plug.

Electricity and Current Events

Ground Rules: You may have often wondered why some outlets have three holes instead of two. The third is for a ground wire. Grounding provides a connecting path to the earth for the electric current, so that in the event that the appliance's wiring becomes damaged and the electricity reaches the metal parts, it would be conducted through the ground wire to the earth. The fuse would then blow, giving evidence of the short. If no grounding were on the appliance when this happened, the current would flow through the metal parts and cause a shock to anyone who touched it. This could be extremely harmful if the person or floor were wet.

If you have an appliance with a three-prong plug that you want to plug into a two-prong outlet, you do it with a three-prong adapter. This has a short wire with a U-shaped terminal which should be placed under the screw of your socket plate. Just loosen the screw, slip the terminal under it, and tighten. This terminal is a substitute for the ground prong.

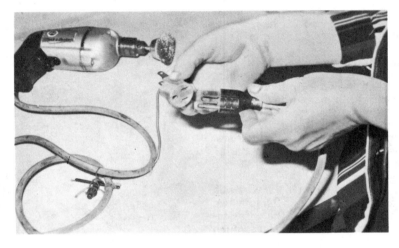

Place three-pronged plug into adapter to use in two-holed outlet.

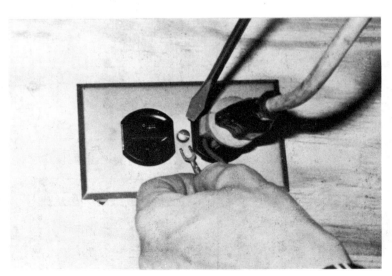

To ground, insert three-prong plug adapter terminal under screw.

Splicing Wires: All wires are covered with insulating material, whether plastic rubber or cloth. Looking head-on at a wire, you see that there are two copper lines running through the center of the insulation. Start by just pulling the two parts of the wire apart until about 2 inches of wire is separated.

Then you *strip* the wire, removing the insulation from about ½ inch of each end. This can be done with a plain pen-knife or a pair of scissors. A tool called a wire stripper has various size notches in the cutting jaws which allow you to cut away *just* the insulation. Since it's easy to cut through the copper, this tool can be of help.

Twist the bared ends of wire so that there are no frayed ends, and then you're ready to attach the wire to another wire, or to a plug, or to a simple device called a crimped terminal. This can be attached to the bared ends of the wires by placing the ends in the terminal barrel and crimping (squeezing or tightening) the barrel. Terminals make for neat, easy installation in many situations.

Another handy invention is the wire nut, which is a small plastic cap to join two wires. Just twist the ends of the wires together and screw on the cap. It's much easier than using electrical tape.

If you must join wires with tape, do it as shown.

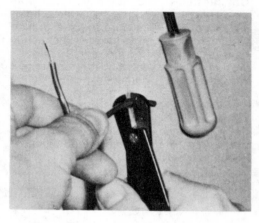

Remove insulation ½ inch from each end.

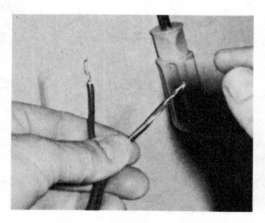

Twist bare wire fibers to form tight strand.

Separate the joined insulated wire strands.

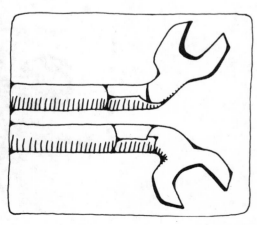

Tighten crimped terminals onto wire ends.

Electricity and Current Events

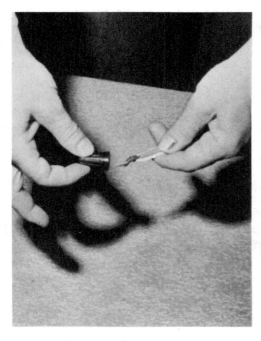

Use a wire nut to connect fixture wires.

Twist tighten wire nut on to joining wires.

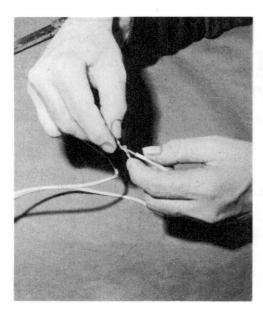

Twist bared wire ends together to splice.

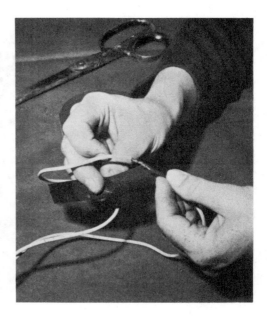

Tape over each bared wire joint to insulate.

Rewiring or Installing a Plug: When possible, use one of the new snap type plugs, which take almost no time at all. Separate the ends of the wire for about ¼ inch. Insert the end, unstripped, into a slot in the plug and snap it closed. Two little metal prongs inside the plug will pierce the wire and make the connection. This plug is suitable for some lamps and lightweight appliances, but any appliance that creates heat, such as an iron or toaster, or uses high wattage, such as a refrigerator, needs a heavy duty plug.

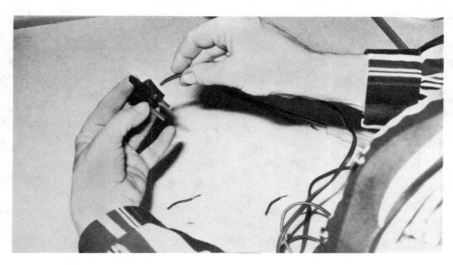

With plug cap held up, insert unstripped wire into the opening on the side.

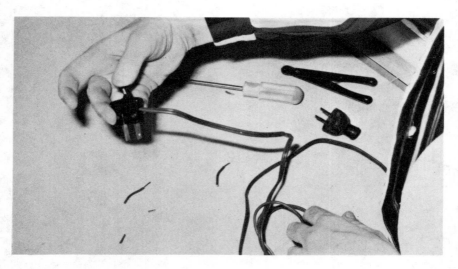

With the wire fully inserted, press plug cap down to close and pierce wire.

Electricity and Current Events

For one of these, take your plug in hand and remove the cardboard cap. With a screwdriver, loosen the two screws at either side of the prongs. Insert your stripped wire through the hole from the side of the plug without prongs. Bring the insulated, separated portion of each half of the wire around, one to each side of a prong. Wind one stripped end around each screw and tighten screw—or attach terminals to each end of bared wire and insert terminals under the screws and tighten. Then replace the cardboard cap.

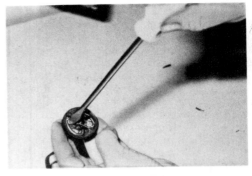

With cardboard removed, loosen screws.

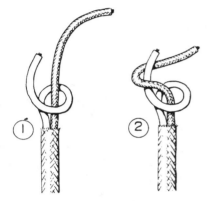

Here is a close-up view of the Underwriters' Knot you must make to wire some plugs.

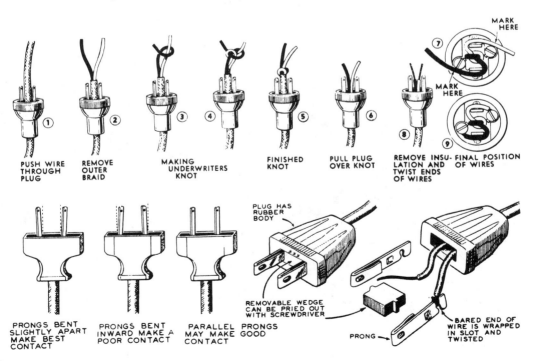

PUSH WIRE THROUGH PLUG

REMOVE OUTER BRAID

MAKING UNDERWRITERS KNOT

FINISHED KNOT

PULL PLUG OVER KNOT

REMOVE INSULATION AND TWIST ENDS OF WIRES

FINAL POSITION OF WIRES

MARK HERE

MARK HERE

PRONGS BENT SLIGHTLY APART MAKE BEST CONTACT

PRONGS BENT INWARD MAKE A POOR CONTACT

PARALLEL PRONGS MAY MAKE GOOD CONTACT

PLUG HAS RUBBER BODY

REMOVABLE WEDGE CAN BE PRIED OUT WITH SCREWDRIVER

PRONG

BARED END OF WIRE IS WRAPPED IN SLOT AND TWISTED

Hooking-up an Extension Cord Socket:
This is just as simple as wiring a plug. Attach a plug to one end of a wire that you've cut to the length you need. On the other end, attach a socket. Open the socket by removing the screw holding it together in back. Separate and strip the ends of your wire. Either attach crimped terminals, as above, or wind wire ends around the screws on opposite sides of the socket. Tighten the screws, and you've got a new outlet . . . all you have to do is plug it into an existing one.

Installing an On-the-Cord Switch: Turning an appliance on or off from a comfortable location is a great convenience, and an on-the-cord switch can make it possible. Separate the switch by loosening and removing the screw or screws holding it together. With the appliance *unplugged,* cut only one of the wires. Lay the wire into the two end slots around the center screw hole. If your switch is the snap together kind there is no need to strip the ends of the cut wire as the prongs will pierce the insulation and make the connection when you replace the other part of the switch and tighten the screw. If your switch is the kind that has two terminal screws, the cut end of the wire must be stripped and wound around each of the screws, and the screws tightened. Re-attach the other half of the switch to close.

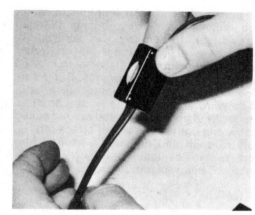
Snap together to make piercing connection.

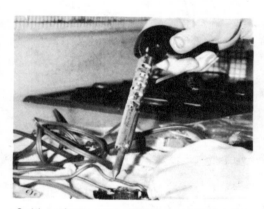
Solder wire to screwless connecting points.

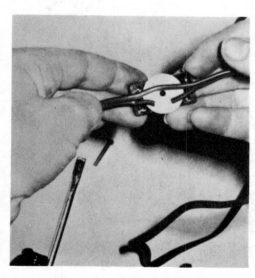
Cut only one wire and lay in switch groove.

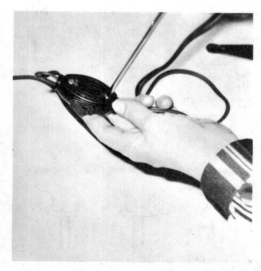
Place screws in cover and tighten to close.

Electricity and Current Events

Attaching a T.V. Antenna: The T.V. antenna sometimes needs to be removed when furniture moving time comes 'round or for cleaning, painting, or moving. Or sometimes the connection breaks loose from constant movement and needs to be properly replaced for clear reception. This is a simple task.

T.V. antenna wire is not attached to an electrical source and has no voltage, but for added precaution and ease of mind, unplug the T.V. while working on it. One end of the antenna wire is attached to the antenna base at the roof or side of the house, and the other end is brought through a window or opening to be attached to the T.V. Strip the ends of the wire coming in from the window. At the rear of the T.V. set you will see a series of sets of screws labeled VHF (Very High Frequency) or UHF (Ultra High Frequency). Your T.V. manual will tell you which is applicable for your area. Either wind each end of the bared wire around one of the pairs of screws and tighten, or attach crimped terminals insert them under screws and tighten.

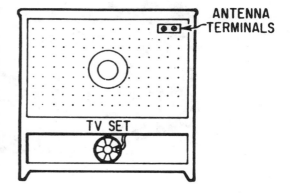

TV SET

ANTENNA TERMINALS

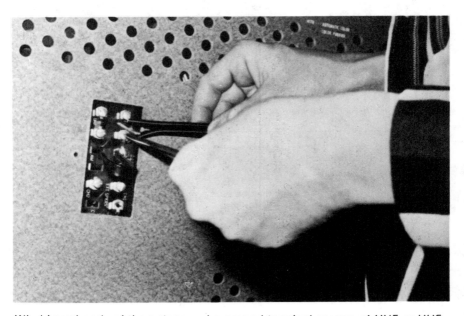

Wind bared ends of the antenna wire around terminal screws of UHF or VHF

Replacing Wires In Appliances: First, be sure the appliance is unplugged! If the cord is frayed or loose at the point where it enters the appliance, cut the cord just below the damaged portion. Take off the covering part of the appliance by locating and removing screws that hold it together.

The terminals where the wire is connected should now be visible. Loosen the screws holding the remainder of the wire to the appliance, and remove and discard the frayed portion. Strip and separate the cut end of the cord and attach wires to the terminal screws. Replace covering parts.

Remove the screw holding the plate enclosing the wire connection.

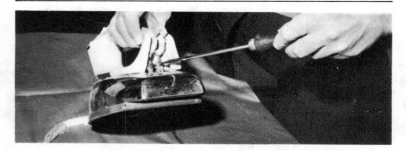

Loosen the screws holding wire terminals to the connecting point.

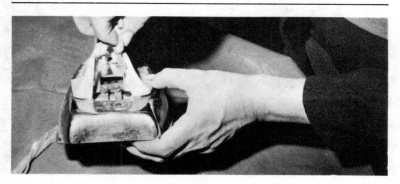

Remove the wire terminals and frayed wire. Replace with new wire.

Electricity and Current Events

That Flickering Fluorescent: Fluorescent lamps are most useful as they provide greater illumination with less wattage consumption and greater life than filament bulbs. They tend to malfunction rather than burn out completely, and some of the malfunctions are correctable.

A flickering fluorescent could be a sign of a weakened tube that needs replacement. If a tested tube flickers, check the socket to be sure that the pins are making firm contact. Squeeze tighten end slots if necessary. Sometimes just turning the tube to sit more firmly in the grooves helps.

Some fluorescents come with a starter which may need replacing. Be sure to replace it with the correct size for your fixture.

Check the contact points at the ends of the bulb. They may need a little sanding to effect sharper contact.

An overloaded circuit will cause fluorescents to malfunction. Check the wattage being consumed on that circuit and remove some appliances if necessary. You may be getting interference from a radio or high frequency appliance on the same circuit.

Try turning the tube end on end. This is a way to reverse the effect of power irregularities in your vicinity.

Be sure tube is clean. Dirt accumulation affects the tube's ability to light.

Lampholders (the brackets that hold the tube) sometimes are broken. They can be easily replaced. *Shut off current.* Loosen the screw holding it in place and disconnect the two wires attaching it. Purchase the same size and model for replacement. Re-connect the two wires and screw holder to fixture.

Low temperatures below 65° will cause fluorescents not to light fully. A warmer room will correct this.

Remove cover from the fluorescent fixture.

Remove the defective starter—Replace.

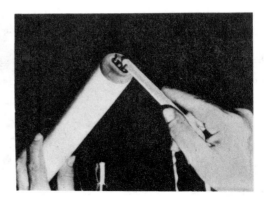

Remove the corrosion from the prongs.

Wiring or Re-wiring a Lamp: Many a lovely liqueur bottle or souvenir memorabilia would make into a lovely lamp if only we knew how. Lamp wiring kits containing all the needed supplies are available at craft stores and some hardware stores. Every lamp is made of four basic parts plus a decorative shade: the *bulb,* which screws into the *socket,* into which is attached the *wire and plug,* all of which is set into the *base* or body.

O.K. now let's start in reverse. If we have a base and body from an old lamp (or the lovely bottle that we spoke of), and a wiring kit, we can proceed to make or re-make a lamp.

Take a length of wire and attach a plug to one end (see *Installing a Plug*). Feed the other end through the hole in the bottom end of the base or bottle. (A hole in a bottle must be drilled carefully. Hold it firmly, as in a vise, and place tape over spot where the hole is to be drilled. Only a high speed electric drill with a sharp bit should be used.) Continue feeding wire on up through the top opening and cork of the kit, and then through the socket base. Strip and separate the wire and attach bared ends under loosened screws of the switch. Tighten the screws, re-assemble the insulation sleeve and outer socket and set onto or screw into the lamp mount or cork mount. Put in a bulb, a shade, plug in and *voilà,* Aladdin has nothing on you!

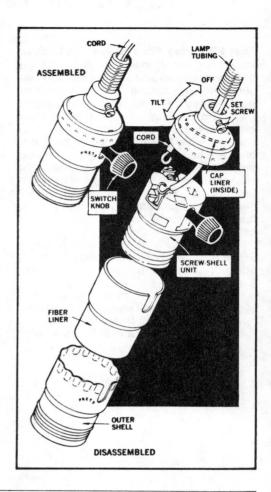

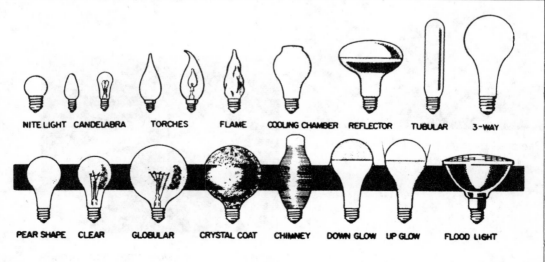

NITE LIGHT · CANDELABRA · TORCHES · FLAME · COOLING CHAMBER · REFLECTOR · TUBULAR · 3-WAY

PEAR SHAPE · CLEAR · GLOBULAR · CRYSTAL COAT · CHIMNEY · DOWN GLOW · UP GLOW · FLOOD LIGHT

Electricity and Current Events

Replacing a Wall Switch: If you flick on the light switch and the light does not go on, first check if the bulb is defective—try it in a working lamp. If a good bulb does not light, the problem is probably in a defective wall switch. Jiggle the switch a bit to shake out any dust that may be blocking connections. If this doesn't work, *shut off electricity at fuse or circuit breaker switch.* Remove the plate cover by taking out the two holding screws. Now remove the screws holding the switch to the junction box in the wall. Pull the switch out of the box. There may be some tension as the wires attached to it are sturdy solid core and do not give easily.

When it is out you will see the wires attached to the terminal screws at top and bottom or sides. Loosen these screws and remove switch. Attach wires to the terminal screws of the new switch. Push switch back into junction box and replace

holding screws, top and bottom. Replace and screw in the wall plate. Re-open fuse or circuit breaker and your light should function.

Be aware of the many new kinds of switches that can be replaced for the old one, e.g. silent switches, lighted switches, and dimmer switches.

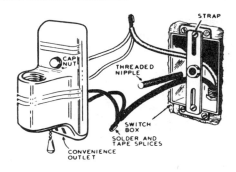

This type fixture is common in bathrooms.

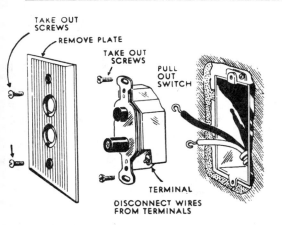

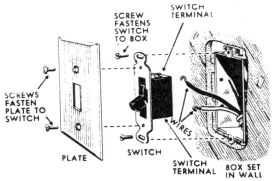

Replacing Wall Sockets: If a socket has been damaged or appliances will not function in it the socket may need to be replaced. *Shut off the current at the fuse box or circuit breaker switch!* Unscrew and remove the outlet face plate. Remove top and bottom screws holding the socket to the junction box in the wall. Pull the socket out of the wall. Loosen the terminal screws on the sides of the socket separating it from the wires. Attach the new

socket, being sure to keep the white wires on one side and the black wires on the other, as on the old switch. You may have to manipulate these wires with pliers to position them properly, since they are heavy and difficult to bend. Tighten terminal screws and replace socket in junction box. Insert the holding screws. Replace the face plate. Open the circuit and test the socket with a lamp.

Installing or Changing Ceiling Fixture:

Perhaps you wish to change the ceiling fixture. *Shut off electricity at fuse or circuit breaker switch.* Remove the screws, bolts or center nut that holds the old fixture in place. Lower the fixture, exposing the wire connection. Carefully note and mark with white adhesive tape which wires the present fixture is attached to. (In basic installation there should be only two, but sometimes additional connections for other wiring is housed here.) Remove electrician's tape or wire nuts to separate these wires. Attach wires of new fixture to the same wires in the ceiling box to which old fixture had been connected. Install fixture nuts or screws, holding fixture to the ceiling box. If the new fixture is of different design, additional mounting brackets may be necessary and should be included with the new fixture, but they can be purchased separately.

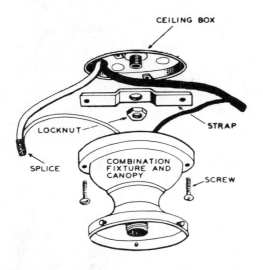

Remove holding screws to release fixture.

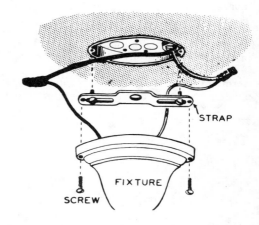

Attach new fixture wires to junction wires.

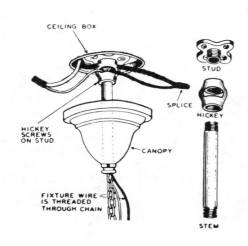

Some fixtures require additional hardware.

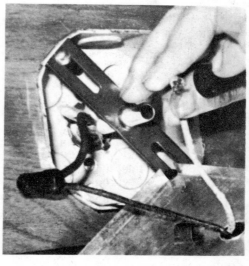

Use wire nuts to attach new fixture wires.

Electricity and Current Events

The Doorbell Doesn't Ring: This is not an unusual problem, and it's also not very difficult. The doorbell system consists of the pushbutton (where the person at your door presses the button to make contact and complete the circuit); the transformer (which changes the house current into the 6, 8, 12, or 24 volts required by your set-up); the bell or chime; and the wiring (which connects all the parts).

There are a few reasons why the bell may not ring. The problem most often lies at the pushbutton, which is subject to constant pressure and corrosive weather conditions. Remove the screws holding the outer covering and you'll see wires connected to two screws. Remove these screws, and, holding wire by the insulated part, allow the two bare ends of wire to touch. (These wires are low voltage, and there is no real danger in handling them —the most you'll get is a tingling jolt if you touch both ends of bared wire at one time.)

Be sure wires are clean of corrosion. You can scrape them clean with an emery board if needed. When bared wires touch, the bell should ring.

If not, the pushbutton itself may need a sanding to bring a sharp contact. If the button spring has no resilience, or if the contact points can not be bent to a position so that they will touch when the button is pushed, you'll need a new bell unit. Then, just attach your clean, bared wire ends to the terminal screws. Test the pushbutton, and you should get a healthy ding-dong! Replace the outer covering.

Very rarely, the transformer burns out and must be replaced. If the bell doesn't ring, and you don't hear a hum at the transformer, it probably needs to be replaced with a new one of the same voltage. *Throw the master switch and remove the fuses before you touch any wires.* Remove the cable that goes to the house current. Replace the connections to the new transformer in exactly the same place and way as you removed them from the old one. Replace the fuse and open the master switch.

The trouble is sometimes a faulty connection of wires at the bell. There may be paint or dust accumulation so that wires aren't making contact. The connection should be secure and clean, so you

may find that the wire ends need sanding . . . get out the emery board.

You should also check that the hammer or clapper reaches to gong. If not, bend it so that it does.

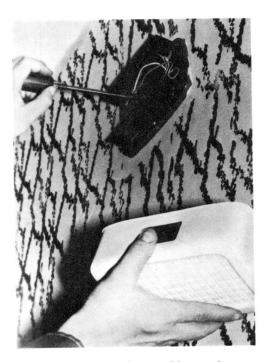

Check firm connection at chime or buzzer.

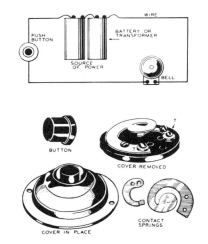

Painless Plumbing

Putting an end to drips, squirts, clogs and clanks.

Many of the plumbing jobs around your home can be done with a twist here, a turn there.

All plumbing problems have to do with water. Knowing the "behind the walls" paths that water takes to and from your sinks, tubs, toilets and washers, will help you in your repair work.

Water comes into your home via a water main from your local water department or company. There's a main shut-off valve which can close off all the incoming water. You will find this in the basement near the ceiling at the street end of the house. This is a cold water line. In order for homes to have both hot and cold water this line connects to a hot water tank and delivers a supply of water. Hot and/or cold lines then continue to your washer, sinks, tubs and toilets. At each of these locations there are shut-off valves. These are metal knobs found under your sinks, along your bathroom walls, over your hot water tank, above your wash tubs.

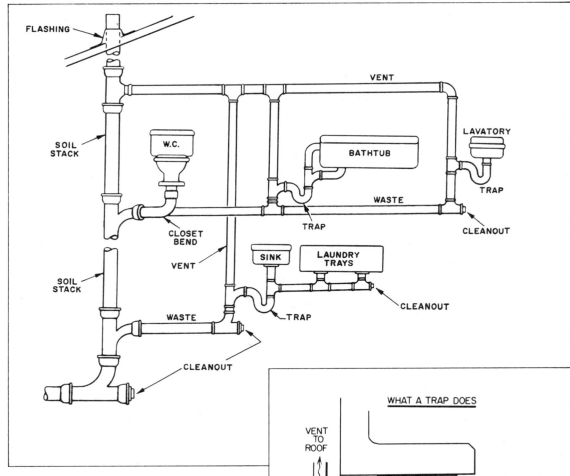

FLASHING

SOIL STACK

SOIL STACK

W.C.

CLOSET BEND

VENT

WASTE

CLEANOUT

VENT

BATHTUB

TRAP

WASTE

LAVATORY

TRAP

CLEANOUT

SINK

LAUNDRY TRAYS

TRAP

CLEANOUT

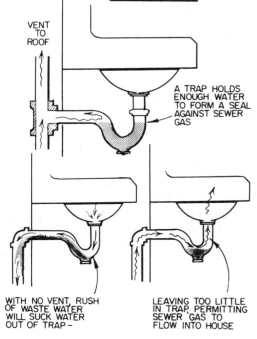

WHAT A TRAP DOES

VENT TO ROOF

A TRAP HOLDS ENOUGH WATER TO FORM A SEAL AGAINST SEWER GAS

WITH NO VENT, RUSH OF WASTE WATER WILL SUCK WATER OUT OF TRAP –

LEAVING TOO LITTLE IN TRAP, PERMITTING SEWER GAS TO FLOW INTO HOUSE

The drainage system is the second half of your plumbing. Water and waste are flushed out of toilets to sewers via soil lines, which are large cast drain pipes. Waste water drains from sinks, tubs and washers via smaller waste pipes which connect to the soil lines. A main clean-out plug is placed just inside the house line, just below floor level, and may be covered by movable boards. Access to this should be kept available, and it should never be permanently covered over. Subsidiary clean-out plugs may be located at other points in your plumbing system, and their handling we leave in the realm of the professional plumber.

Clogged Bathroom Sink: Often this becomes clogged or slow draining. Pull up and take out the basin plug and remove hair and gunk that is embedded around the neck and bottom of the stopper. An open end of wire coat hanger, bent into a hook, inserted into the drain hole will pull up any more that has collected and matted under the stopper. A treatment with a commercial drain cleaner will clear the rest of the line.

Release holding mechanism and then pull out sink plug from drain.

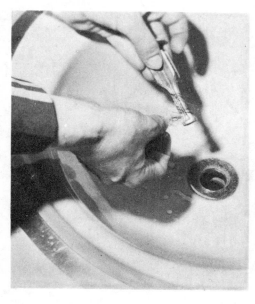

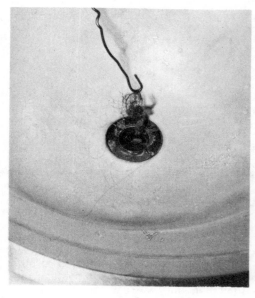

Loosen and remove hairs and gunk.   *Insert a wire hook to pull up more mess.*

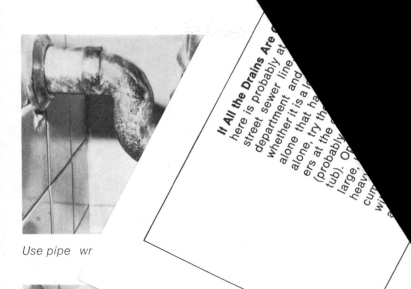

Use pipe wr

If All the Drains Are
here is probably at
street sewer line
department and
whether it is a l
alone, try th
ers at the
(probably
tub). O
large,
heav
cum
wi

With pail to catch water, remove trap plug.

Loosen and remove collar holding trap.

nut lo
J-shaped p
traps have th
the trap itself by lo
the two joint collars tha
Set a basin below to catch ι.
will flow out. With a pipe wrenc..
trap plug counter-clockwise. Wrap a
sive tape or a piece of cloth around the
plug to protect it and prevent chewing up
the chrome edges. When the plug is out,
let fall out into the basin what will. Then,
with rubber-gloved fingers, pull out any
lodged pieces. The coat hanger hook
may be of further assistance or you may
have to insert a *snake* through the plug
hole or the drain opening to clear further
down the line. A garden hose could be
substituted for a snake by inserting it as
far as it will go into the pipe and turning
the hose's water pressure on full force. Be
prepared for a backsplash if the water
pressure does not move the blockage.

When replacing the drain plug or joint
collars, coat them with *pipe compound*
(a plumbing sealant) to avoid leakage
from a bad seal. When finished with
snake and tools, clean, dry and wipe
them down with oil to prevent rust.

Clogged: The trouble the main drain or the Check with the sewer neighbors to determine cal problem or your house s the trouble. If it is yours e snake or commercial clean-drain closest to the main drain a basement shower or laundry ening the main drain requires a eavy wrench and pounding with a hammer. When opened, all the ac-ulated water and waste in the lines l gush out. This is a job to relegate to professional plumber or drain-clearing company.

Brush pipe joint cement on to threads.

Wind plumber's cord around pipe threads.

Leaks at Incoming Pipe Joints: Tighten the joint with a wrench. If this does not help, shut valve at next opening before this joint and loosen the joint. Place *plumber's cord* and pipe compound around the threads in the same direction as the collar threads on. Re-tighten, let dry, open the valve, and test it.

If you don't have the tools to open the joint, or you can't get it open, a long-term temporary measure that works is to shut the valve to allow the joint to dry. Then wind on plumber's cord and apply leak stopper at the seam, or pack epoxy cement around the tightened, dried joint following package directions.

Replace corded pipe on joint and tighten.

Painless Plumbing

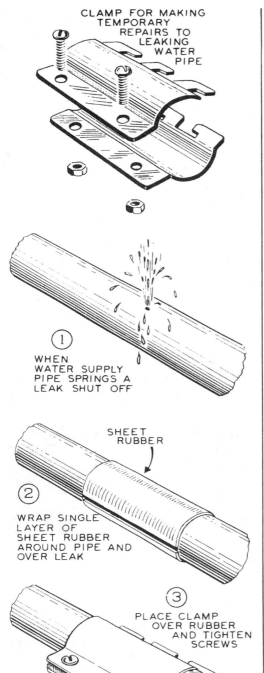

CLAMP FOR MAKING TEMPORARY REPAIRS TO LEAKING WATER PIPE

① WHEN WATER SUPPLY PIPE SPRINGS A LEAK SHUT OFF

SHEET RUBBER

② WRAP SINGLE LAYER OF SHEET RUBBER AROUND PIPE AND OVER LEAK

③ PLACE CLAMP OVER RUBBER AND TIGHTEN SCREWS

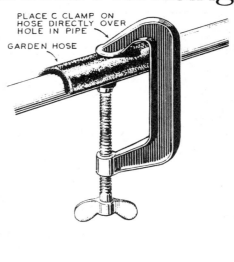

PLACE C CLAMP ON HOSE DIRECTLY OVER HOLE IN PIPE

GARDEN HOSE

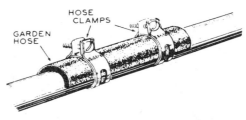

HOSE CLAMPS

GARDEN HOSE

Pipe Leak, Not at a Joint: If a leak is found along the length of a supply pipe, shut off the water supply. Calculate the size of the pipe by measuring circumference (around the outside of the pipe):

Circumference—Pipe size

Circumference	Pipe size
1.315	1 inch
1.05	¾ inch
.084	½ inch

Correct pipe clamp can be purchased for pipe size. A piece of sheet rubber comes with each clamp. Wrap the sheet rubber around the pipe with the center over the leaking area. Separate the clamp pieces and place them around pipe over the rubber sheet. Screw tightly so that the rubber is firmly compressed. Leak should be controlled. Pipe may in time have to be replaced, but this can be a long term temporary correction. For emergency measure if no clamps can be obtained, a piece of inner tube or garden hose held tightly in place with twisted tie wire will function for short term.

Leaky Trap Pipe: The trap pipe (that P- S- or J-shaped pipe under your sink) is made of thin-walled metal and often wears out or develops leaks. Sometimes these can be patched with epoxy cement or leak stopper. Follow package directions and fill cracks or holes. If, after drying, leak has not been corrected, the trap pipe needs to be replaced. Have a basin ready to catch accumulated water. Protect the hexagonal ring by wrapping it with tape. With a monkey wrench, loosen it with counter-clockwise turns. The rings will slip up and the trap will slip out. Bring it to a hardware or pipe supply store and purchase one of same size and shape. Many come in pre-packaged kits with new gaskets. Slip the new trap and gasket in place and attach the hexagonal ring, applying pipe compound to threads. Hand tighten with clockwise turns, and then tighten further with the wrench.

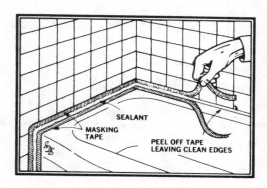

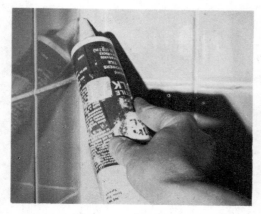

Apply caulk to tub or shower tile joint.

Leaks at Sink, Tub, and Shower Seams: Water leaking from tub, shower stall, sink and counter surfaces can damage walls and ceilings below. In order to prevent this damage all tubs, stalls, sink and counter joints should be well caulked. Many latex compounds now come in tubes subject to finger pressure so that no special tool is necessary. Most caulk comes white and can be painted over to match. Some now come pre-colored to match bathroom tiles.

Scrape out all old dried caulk. In order to perform a neat job, place masking tape on the wall and tub or counter surface about ¼ to ½ inch from joint. Squeeze out caulking, running along the joint line, leaving no spaces or air bubbles. Firm in and smooth with a wooden pop stick or back end of wooden spoon. When caulking is dry, remove masking tape.

With wrench remove existing shower head.

Clogged Faucets and Showerheads: Most modern faucets come equipped with a strainer or aerator to give an even flow of water and avoid splashing. These often get clogged with rust, sand and grit, which reduce the flow of water. The aerator or strainer needs to be removed and cleaned or replaced. Try turning it counter-clockwise by hand. If it doesn't give, protect the surface with one or two layers of adhesive tape and apply a small wrench or large pliers until you loosen it. Unthread and remove it. Catch all the parts that come loose with it. They should include a washer, one or two screen cylinders, maybe a metal holed plate and the threaded cylinder. Rinse out the parts. If the washer or screen is damaged, replace them or the whole aerator by simply screwing in a new one with a clockwise motion.

Showerheads tend to clog in the same manner as faucet heads. They are attached either by the same kind of threaded collar or by a screw. Release and remove either of these and rinse through the shower nozzle from the reverse side. Re-assemble and attach.

In the goose-neck type of extended swivel shower head there is a soft-core metal center which eventually breaks from constant bending. It then falls into the shower head, locks the adjustment handle and clogs the water flow. Remove the nozzle from the extended pipe by holding the pipe with one wrench and turning the nozzle with another. You may need another set of hands if it does not give easily. When you get it apart, the metal rod will slide out, or else jiggle the flexible tube to help it along. Discard it and re-assemble the nozzle head. It will no longer be flexible but it will be extended and usable.

You could also replace this piece or your original simple shower head by removing it from the stationary shower water pipe extending from the wall with a wrench and attaching a new one, which will come complete with attaching washers, gaskets and couplings.

Install a new flexible combination model.

Faucet Leaks: Locate the shut-off valve either under the sink or on the wall near the toilet tank, and shut off water supply. Remove the screw in the top of the faucet knob. Pry off the knob cap with a screwdriver. It may need a bit of jiggling but it will pry up.

Now with either an adjustable wrench or the proper size flat wrench, loosen the packing with counter-clockwise turns. With additional hand turns the whole valve stem will unscrew, and reveal, on its bottom, a washer held in place by a brass screw. Remove this screw and washer and replace with new washer of same size.

While you have the valve stem out, check the condition of the valve seat (the hole that the valve stem fits into). If it has corrosion, grit or burrs it will not allow a tight seal. There is an inexpensive re-smoothing tool you can get while you're buying your washers, with instructions for its simple use in correcting your valve seat.

Leaks at a spout connection are usually from a loose connecting nut, which you can wrench-tighten, or loosen and remove it to check the O-ring or packing that you will find there. Replace if its condition is causing the leak. Replace spout and tighten connecting nut.

1. Turn off incoming water supply valve.

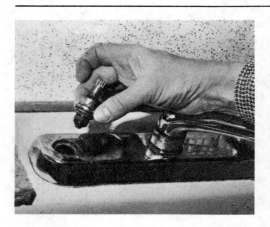

4. With hand turns remove faucet bonnet.

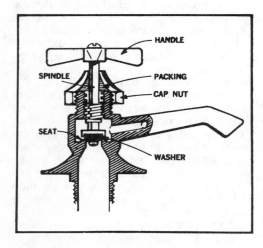

A cross section view of a basic faucet.

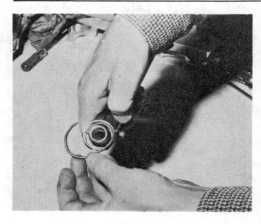

7. Wind packing on threads of spout joint.

Painless Plumbing

2. Remove head screw and pry off handle.

3. With wrench loosen faucet packing nut.

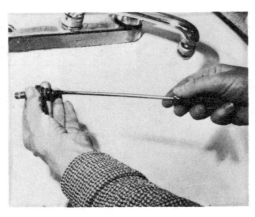

5. Remove the washer screw and washer.

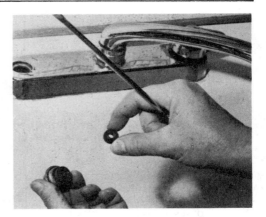

6. Replace with new washer of same size.

8. Loosen and remove spout aerator nozzle.

9. Replace with a new screen and gasket.

Replacing a Toilet Seat: Many comfortable, colorful, artistic, and humorous toilet seats are on the market which can make life and your bathroom more decorative, pleasant, and fun filled. Why not change the old for a new? They come in standard sizes and equipped with their own hinges and nuts (although additional washers may be necessary). Just unscrew the two wing nuts or bolts, using a wrench and holding the hinge of the old seat. Attach the new one by inserting the hinge bolts through the accommodating holes. Apply washers, thread on the nuts and tighten. Simply pretty-fied!

Curing Water Hammer, (Those Rumbling Pipes): Water hammer is that banging vibration that is sometimes heard after shutting faucets.

Cause One is vibrating pipes. If no U-brackets support the water pipes along the ceiling beams in the basement, install them and insert pieces of felt between them and the pipes to cushion the vibration.

Cause Two is the loss of an air cushion which was built into the plumbing system to cushion the shock of sudden water turn off. The multi-phase cure is aimed at getting air into the pipes. With toilet tanks full, shut off valves leading to them. Close the main valve for incoming water supply. Open the highest and lowest faucets in the house to drain all the water out of the lines. When all water stops flowing, close the two faucets and re-open the main valve. The refilling of the empty lines should re-establish a normal air cushion.

If neither of the cures helps, have your water pressure checked. If it is too high you may need a pressure reducing valve, or your home may not have air cushion chambers built-in and you may need to have them installed.

Air cushion chambers stabilize water flow. To adjust hammer, drain and refill line.

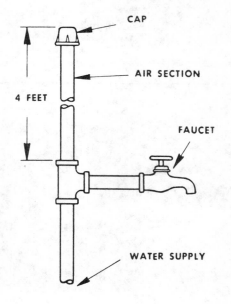

CAP

AIR SECTION

4 FEET

FAUCET

WATER SUPPLY

Painless Plumbing

Radiator Won't Heat: Be sure the open-close valve knob at the bottom is turned to the open position. If it is, the trouble may be in the *air valve.* Here's how the air valve works: the cold air is pushed through that tiny hole in the top by the pressure of the incoming steam. When the radiator is filled with steam, the rise in temperature automatically closes the valve and keeps the steam from escaping into the room.

Here's how it doesn't work: sometimes because of rust, grit, dirt or corrosion, this valve becomes stuck closed, so the cold air cannot get out. The radiator is said to be *air bound* and the heated steam cannot get into it.

To fix it, close the radiator shut-off valve. When cool, unscrew the air valve by turning it counter-clockwise. Tap it against a hard surface to loosen dirt. Force air through the threaded end by blowing or using a football or bicycle pump. If air goes through, re-install it. If air doesn't go through, boil it in baking soda for about ½ hour, or soak it in kerosene overnight and rinse out rust and scale. If the valve does not release and allow air passage, purchase and install a new valve.

If the air valve sputters steam or water it should be replaced. In hot water systems just open valve with a turnkey or pliers and allow air out until water flows. Then close. The radiator should now be ready to go back to work.

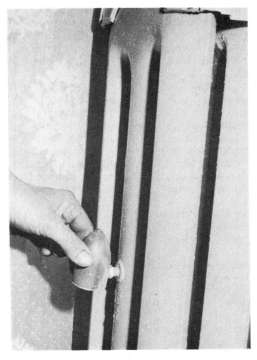

Remove radiator valve to unclog or replace.

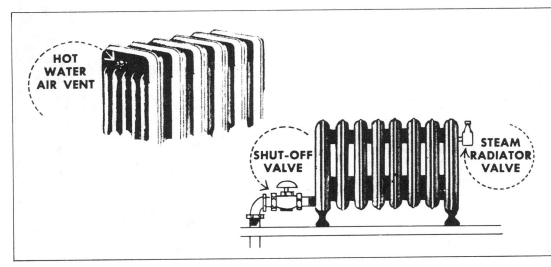

Clanking Radiator: The return flow system is another area where troubles arise. When the heated steam gives off its heat to the radiators and room, the cooler steam condenses to form water and should flow back to the furnace boiler via this system to be reheated. If the shut-off valve in steam systems is partially opened, the pressure of the steam forcing against the valve and the slowed movement of the air out through the air valve can cause banging. Keep the shut-off valve closed all the way or opened all the way.

Another cause for that clanking is a sagging floor, or the building's settling, which may sometimes cause radiators to slant slightly so that the side opposite the shut-off valve is lower. In this case the condensed water lays in the radiator and does not flow back to the boiler. The sudden surge of steam when the heat comes up again sends this cooled water banging around in the radiator. To fix it, place small wooden wedges under the legs at the far end of the radiator (away from the shut-off valve) to bring the radiator at least to level and preferably slightly slanted towards the shut-off valve and return pipe. Condensed water will drain off and eliminate that bang and gurgle. Sometimes all four legs need to be propped slightly to bring entire radiator slightly above the pipe connection to the shut-off valve.

Adjust the radiator level with wood chocks.

Leaky Radiator Shut-off Valve: If the shut-off valve leaks and spurts water around stem area, tighten the packing nut just under stem a couple of turns with pipe wrench or adjustable wrench. If it still leaks, shut the valve and let it cool, then loosen that nut and slide it up along the stem to gain access to the part it was threaded onto. Wind packing or plumbers cord around the threads of the shaft and re-tighten the nut.

To do this job in hot water systems you would have to drain the water out of the radiator to below the level of this joint before opening the packing nut.

Tighten the packing nut to eliminate leaks.

Painless Plumbing

Toilet Tank Basics: What's supposed to happen is that when the handle is pressed, it lifts the horizontal bar, pulling up the tank ball, and allowing water which was in the tank to gush out to the bowl. As the tank empties, the tank ball sinks slowly back to reseal the opening. As the water level drops in the tank, the float ball drops with it. The arm attached to the descended float ball opens the ballcock valve and intake water starts to refill the tank. The float ball then rises with the incoming water. When it reaches the proper level (about 1-1½ inches from top of overflow tube) the float ball arm resumes a hori-zontal position and closes the ballcock intake valve. The tank is now ready for the next flush.

When the system doesn't work, it can be because of any of a number of problems. Before going into any of the symptoms and cures, note that it may be necessary to shut off the water supply to work. Turn the shut-off valve (which is attached to the pipe extending from the wall) completely clockwise. Or flush and then prop a length of board or a hanger under the float ball rod to hold it in the up position so that no water will enter the tank.

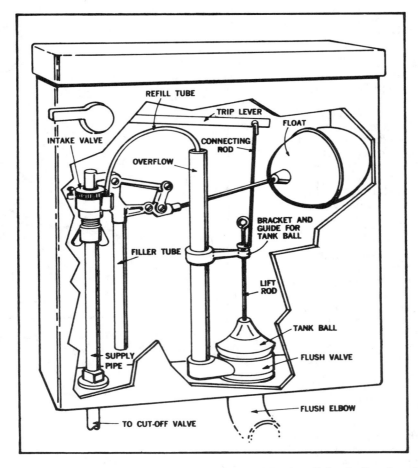

Tank Doesn't Fill: The valve controlling the water supply may not be fully opened, or the ballcock valve is closing too soon.

To cure the first problem, bend the float rod down to a straighter position until the refill water reaches about 1 inch below the refill tube. If the ballcock valve is the problem, it can be adjusted by hand (by loosening the ring on the side facing the overflow tube) to allow more water in. Tightening it allows less water in.

Water Flows Continuously: This is sometimes due to poor seating of the tank ball, and is usually quieted temporarily by jiggling the handle. Normally, the tank ball is drawn by the incoming water pressure to sit vertically, sealing the opening. if there is too much play in the stem, or too loose a chain, the ball may land off-center.

Flush the tank, and with the cover off observe the seating of the ball. If it is off-center, take up the slack by opening up the link of chain attached to the horizontal arm (pry it open with a screwdriver) and re-attaching a link further along the chain, or if you've got a stem and not a chain, simply bend the top of the stem to make the stem just long enough to allow proper seating.

Another cause for continuous water flow is a corroded outlet rim on the tank ball. Flush and keep supply of water out of the tank. Dry the porcelain rim and clean it off with an old toothbrush, smoothing the surface with emery cloth. Then check seating. If the tank ball is so far gone that it can no longer hold a tight seal, empty the tank, unscrew the ball by holding it and turning the stem. Attach a new ball of the same kind. If corrosion doesn't allow easy separation of stem from ball, bend the stem back and forth until it breaks off. Then replace the stem and the ball.

Sometimes, because the ballcock valve doesn't close, water continuously runs through the overflow tube. Since the valve is controlled by the flotation assembly, that's where the adjustment has to be made. If it's the rod that's causing difficulties, bend it to change the position of the float ball. If the trouble is with the float ball itself, which sometimes gets punctured and refuses to float, remove it by turning it counter-clockwise, and replace it with a new plastic or Styrofoam one.

Seldom, the ballcock valve washer becomes defective and needs to be replaced. It is located on the top of the ballcock mechanism, inside the plunger. Remove the screw holding the lever arm to the plunger. Lift up and slide off the plunger. The washer to be replaced is on the bottom, held either by a screw or snaps. Remove it, replace it, and reassemble the mechanism.

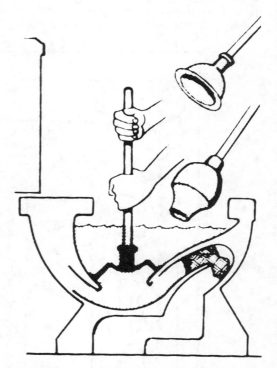

Dislodge clogging cause in the toilet bowl with plumber's friend or force cup action.

Toilet Water Rises Dangerously High: After flushing, instead of going down the water is often blocked in the bowl. This problem has nothing to do with the tank —it's a drainage difficulty. Commercial drain cleaners should *not* be used in toilets. Use the force cup plunger placed over the opening where the water would go down and use the same pumping action described for a sink drain. Close movement will keep the waste water from splashing over excessively.

If this does not dislodge whatever was blocking the passage of water you may have to use the snake or auger. It's a messy job. I suggest putting a long plastic bag over your arm and securing it with large rubber bands. Then push the snake end or auger into the hole and around the bend as far as it will go, and then turn. The water should go down as the blockage is removed.

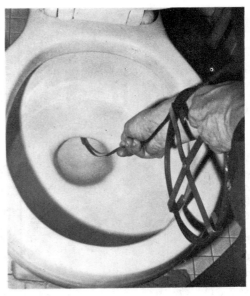

Push length of snake into the bowl opening.

Insert coiled snake head in toilet bowl.

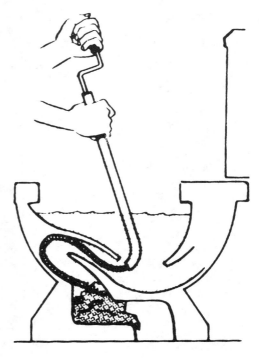

Push, twist, turn, and force snake length against lodged substance to loosen clog.

Flawless Floors

The lowdown on what you've got to stand on.

Beautiful and durable hexagonal tiles such as these come in a wide variety of sizes.

Changing the look of your floor, or making repairs, isn't nearly as bad a job as it may seem. There may be a few steps involved, but the results are fabulous, and well worth the effort.

Refinishing a Wood Floor: If the finish of a wood floor is worn or discolored, or if you wish to have a different shade, it's time to refinish.

Preparation and removal of the old finish. If the floor is in good condition the finish can be removed with solvent type finish removers, which can be brushed on and, after required standing time, removed with a scraper or steel wool disc on a floor polisher. Several applications may be necessary, or you may resort to sanding.

For sanding, counterset all nail heads below the wood surface and fill holes with wood putty. Remove baseboard molding, being careful to pry slowly in order to get them off in one piece. Fasten any loose boards. Fill splits or spaces with plastic wood. Remove all furniture, draperies, pictures, etc., as the wood dust tends to get on everything. Close doors to other rooms and open all available windows. Sanding machine can be rented by the day from most large hardware stores. A drum sander is an upright push-handle type machine used for the overall floor area. A disc edge sander is a smaller hand-held machine, used for baseboard edge areas, stair treads and other close work.

The best sanding is done in three operations with different grades of sandpaper: 1) 3½ (20 grit), 2) 1½ (40 grit),

Counterset all nail heads below surface.

3) 2/0 (100 grit). Make a slow walking pass with the machine in the direction of the floorboards and back over the same area, each pass overlapping the previous one by 2 to 3 inches. *Do not stop* while the machine is running, as it will gouge into one area, damaging the floor.

When first sanding is done with both drum sander and disc sander, change sandpaper and proceed to second and then to third, increasing the pace of your walk slightly each time. Then remove all dust from the room including ledges, door and window frames with a vacuum cleaner and dry brush. The new finish should be applied as quickly as possible after sanding to avoid dirt or foot marks or moisture to affect freshly sanded wood.

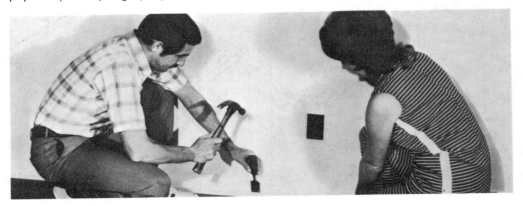

For refinishing a wood floor or replacing flooring, you may have to remove moldings.

Finishes are most easily applied with a long-handled roller. While shellacs and varnishes are old stand-bys, the new urethanes last twice as long. Some come in two-part mixtures, which you must combine before applying. Others are one-part mixtures, which can be applied directly from the can. They come in clear, simulated mahogany, oak, cherry, and light walnut stains. Two to three coats with a light sanding or steel wool rubbing in between makes for gymnasium or bowling alley ruggedness.

Pre-finished Wood Squares: The elegance of parquet type flooring of yesteryear is hardly installed with today's mass building methods. It can again be achieved by laying pre-finished wood squares in alternating patterns.

Remove all baseboard before starting. Establish a square line depending on the size and shape of your room, and the direction in which you wish to install the blocks—straight line or diagonal. Apply mastic with a serrated trowel to only as large an area as you can reach to work on. Let mastic set for the time allotted in the directions on the can. In laying each block, see that the edge of the block aligns with the squared line, not the tongue or groove protrusion. Add tiles pyramid fashion around the first tile, to maintain squared line, fitting tongues and grooves and alternating squares to create design. Continue fitting additional tiles pyramid style until area is covered. If placing tiles on a diagonal, cut necessary triangular shapes out of blocks to fit against wall. Replace baseboards or install new molding of proper size and stain to match your new floor.

Apply mastic to small area; set squares.

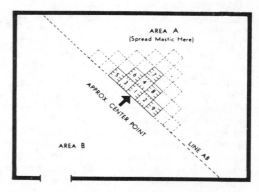

Follow pyramid pattern in setting squares.

Wood squares create look of parquet floor.

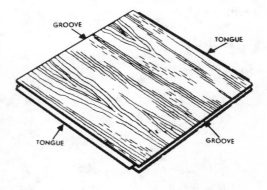

Tongue in groove finish makes a tight fit.

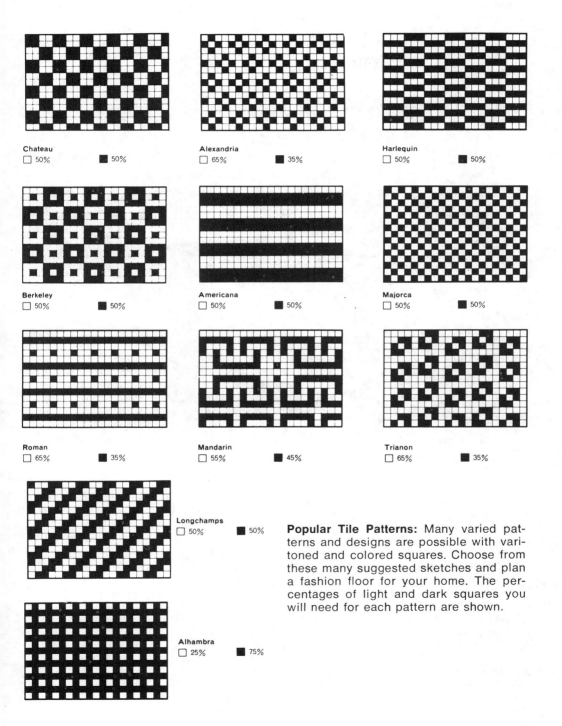

Chateau
☐ 50%   ■ 50%

Alexandria
☐ 65%   ■ 35%

Harlequin
☐ 50%   ■ 50%

Berkeley
☐ 50%   ■ 50%

Americana
☐ 50%   ■ 50%

Majorca
☐ 50%   ■ 50%

Roman
☐ 65%   ■ 35%

Mandarin
☐ 55%   ■ 45%

Trianon
☐ 65%   ■ 35%

Longchamps
☐ 50%   ■ 50%

Alhambra
☐ 25%   ■ 75%

Popular Tile Patterns: Many varied patterns and designs are possible with varitoned and colored squares. Choose from these many suggested sketches and plan a fashion floor for your home. The percentages of light and dark squares you will need for each pattern are shown.

Flawless Floors

Installing Floor Tiles: Tools you will need for this are a serrated trowel, heavy-duty scissors or tin snips, contour gauge, pencil, measuring tape, and an awl or icepick.

Floor preparation. It is necessary to start with a smooth, clean, even surface. Tile can be laid directly over the concrete. Wood floors should be smooth and tight-jointed. If they are loose, re-nail. Pound all nails down tight. If there are ridges or slight spaces, a felt liner or a layer of masonite is highly recommended. If you are placing tiles over a previous linoleum floor that is intact, it will act as the necessary base padding.

An easy way to get the luxurious effect of parquet is with self-adhesive vinyl tiles.

Kinds of Tile. Asphalt tile can be used directly over concrete or wood but are hard, noisy and brittle and crack easily on impact, or during handling in installation, or from contact with cold weather. They need to be heated for resilience in installation.

Vinyl tiles are easiest to handle. They cut easily, are resilient and are not affected by weather conditions. They come in many colors and patterns.

Self-adhesive tiles come pre-glued with a paper backing which is easily peeled off when you are ready to apply them. No adhesive is necessary. These might be a little more expensive, but they're much more convenient.

Where to start. Many manuals recommend establishing centering lines from either wall and starting at the exact mid point of the room so that cut tiles will be evenly spaced at edges. In large open rooms this method could be used, but it is most important in smaller or odd-shaped rooms, measuring so as not to have less-than-half tiles at edges.

If using peel n' stick tiles, start at squared line, peel backing and place tile (do not slide) on lines. Continue placing tiles, fitting edges before sticking down. Press each tile firmly in place.

Combining vinyl tile patterns is a sure-fire way to brighten-up a kitchen.

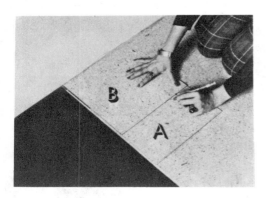

Place tile B at wall; draw cut line on A.

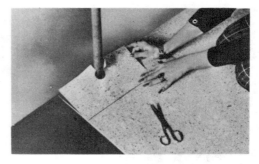

For such shapes, cut paper pattern first.

To fit partial tiles at straight edges, place a tile directly on top of the last full tile before the space. Then place a third tile against the wall over the space and on top of the second tile. Hold firmly and mark with a pencil, or score with a knife or awl, the line on the second tile where this third tile reaches. Cut the second tile along this line. It should then form the proper fit to the space.

For odd-shaped curved edges or around pipes, measure distance needed for the odd tile from the straight tile joint. Transfer this to a paper square the size of the tile. Cut and fit, forming a paper pattern of the odd shape. Transfer the pattern to the tile and cut with scissor. A contour gauge is available for this purpose which you press against the desired shape, forcing tiny metal prongs to assume that contour. This is then transferred to the tile to be cut.

If you are using adhesive for your tile, start at square line and apply adhesive onto one-quarter of the floor. Let it set. Start laying tiles from the square line to outer edge. Proceed to succeeding quarters, laying all full tiles before cutting for edges, as above. Wipe excess adhesive as you go.

Plain colors in strips can be used to create custom effects. Checkerboard or pattern designs should be laid out on graph paper to scale and followed as a floor plan while laying tiles.

Square off chalk line from center of room.

Lay out tiles to determine edge spacing.

Apply adhesive to quarter area at a time.

Install tiles, doing the edge spaces last.

Flawless Floors

Azrock

Beautiful custom designed effects can be achieved by the planning and installing of contrasting or matching color strips, or accent pieces such as the dark squares shown.

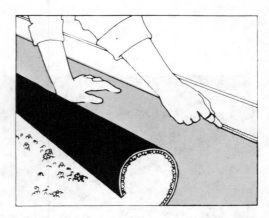

1. *Mark a chalk line at the edge of the floor to transfer to backing of the carpet.*

Installing Carpet Tiles and Seamless Carpet: Carpeting has moved into the realm of the do-it-yourselfer with the advent of carpet tiles and double faced foam tape. Tiles can be laid on any floor, including concrete. They come in a wide variety of textures, colors, materials and even shapes. The foam pad backing can be easily cut with a scissor or exacto knife, to cut out and insert your own shapes (Armstrong Cork Company offers a package of twelve different patterns free to anyone who writes to the company's office in Lancaster, Pennsylvania).

To lay the tiles just criss-cross the floor with double faced adhesive tape so that the cross falls on about the center of each square row. Some squares have a self-adhesive bonding system and no taping is necessary. Many patterns can be worked out, from the standard checkerboard to sequential stripes, diamonds, etc. Press each tile in place according to your pattern, fitting neatly to the preceding tile. Cut to fit at edges as with vinyl tile.

Wall to wall shag carpet is now also easily installed by the average home maker with new "seamless" stick-down carpet. It is bonded to a built-in pad of foam latex, and is easily cut with a scissor. It comes in 6-foot widths, so it is easy to handle. The advantage of the roll over the tile is there are fewer seams. The carpet is positioned to overlap the wall where fitting into doorways or odd corners, and then cut to fit floor joint. Butting edges are joined on the bottom with double faced tape. The shaggy texture of the carpet meshes and blends to make the overall job look like a single piece. Do it yourself!

4. *Roll out second strip, wrinkle-free, and butt against first strip at the seam edge.*

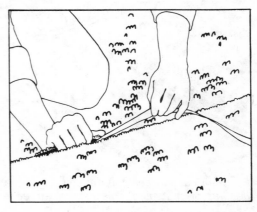

7. *Roll second strip of carpet on taped line, remove backing, clear away fibers, press.*

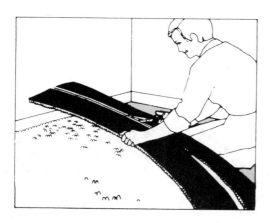

2. Roll carpet against chalk mark and pick up on backing. Cut along this line.

3. When installing two or more widths, roll first length allowing extra at wall.

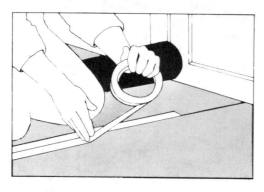

5. Apply double face carpet tape to both sides of joint line marked on the floor.

6. Roll carpet onto taped joint line and remove tape backing. Press down firmly.

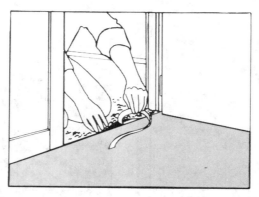

8. At doorway openings, apply one strip of tape under the carpet edge and press.

Flawless Floors

Correcting Squeaky Floors and Stairs:
Shaking talcum powder into squeaky floor boards, or spraying silicone or powdered graphite or even a squirt of liquid soap can be temporary corrections. A coat of penetrating floor sealer may be more permanent. Brush with the grain, wiping the excess against the grain. A final light stroke with the grain after a day of drying may solve your problem.

If the flooring has separated from the sub-floor, drill holes and drive in nails at an angle. Finish by countersinking nails and using wood filler on top of holes.

If squeaks persist and seem to stem from sagging joists, it will be necessary to get at underflooring construction via the basement ceilings, which may be a more extensive job than we want to undertake.

Stairs that squeak are usually caused by the treads rubbing against the risers, which have separated because of inadequate nailing. If there is a molding between the tread and the riser, remove it. With a heavy weight on the tread, drill at an angle through the tread into the riser. Nail down with 10D resin coated nails. Re-attach molding and remove the weight. You should now have silent stairs.

A squirt of silicone spray eases squeaks.

A bit of talcum helps squeaky floorboards.

Renail riser to tread to stop stair squeak.

Rescuing Sick Furniture

Making your furnishings as good as new.

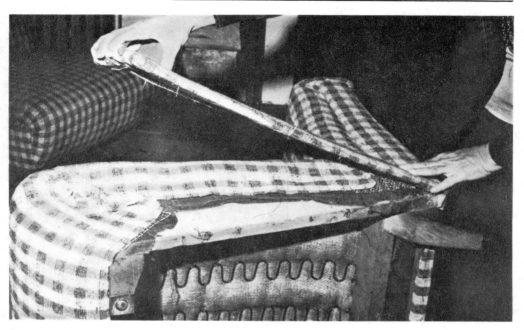

Save money on reupholstering by doing it yourself. Start by prying off chair's side panels.

Sometimes a piece of furniture may be so wobbly or scarred that you think you'd rather throw it away than go through the trouble and expense of fixing it. But here's some good news—many of these can be given new life and beauty easily and at very little cost.

Sick Chairs: Often chairs are misused as step ladders, foot rests, balance beams or stack shelves. This misuse usually leads to the breaking of one or more of the rungs, leaving part of the dowel in the holes. With a drill bit slightly smaller than the dowel diameter, drill out the center of the wood stuck in the hole, being careful not to drill too far and cut into the leg. Soak the hole with vinegar to soften the glue. Measure the diameter of the hole and the length of the space between the legs, plus the depth of the two holes, and purchase new dowel of these dimensions. Mark off on the dowel the depth of the holes. With chisel or penknife taper ends from that line. Cross-score ends with a knife for better glue adhesion. Insert glue and dowel, and tie cord around legs of chair to hold tightly until dry. Refinish rung to match the chair.

For loose dowels, loose legs, or loose joints, clean the hole or joint opening and the dowel and the leg edge with vinegar to remove glue. Place several thin layers of tissue over tip of inserting piece. Spread glue over tissue and into hole. Insert piece and tie or clamp into place. Let dry.

If screw holes have become loose and don't hold, fill them with plastic wood. When dry, re-insert screw.

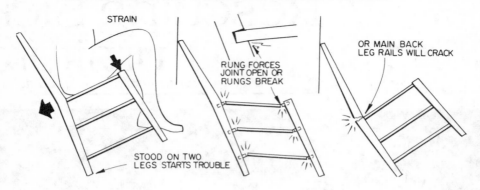

STRAIN

RUNG FORCES
JOINT OPEN OR
RUNGS BREAK

OR MAIN BACK
LEG RAILS WILL CRACK

STOOD ON TWO
LEGS STARTS TROUBLE

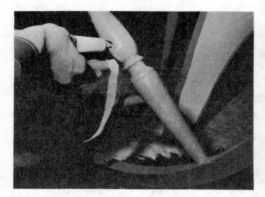

Apply tissue strip; glue to end of rung.

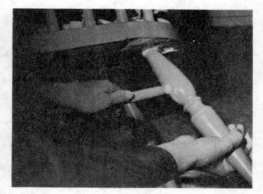

Insert rung into hole; then push together.

You may need to buy a new dowel that fits.

Protect legs and rope-tie till glue dries.

Rescuing Sick Furniture

Recovering Worn Seats (and Folding Tables): Padded chair seats become frayed or faded and just beg for new covers from time to time. Turn chair upside-down, resting the seat on the table, and remove the screws holding the seat in place. Carefully remove the old covering and use this as a pattern for measuring and cutting the new fabric. If the padding is lumpy or worn down, replace it with batting or foam rubber padding. Place the new fabric, cut to size, face down on the table with the seat face down on it. Space the material evenly all the way around. With small carpet tacks or a staple gun, attach straight sides, pulling tightly at opposite edges for a tight, smooth fit. Gently ease the corners into short folds on the underside, accomplishing smoothed curved fit on the right side. Continue tacking all corners in this fashion. Trim away any bulky fabric at corners and excess along straight lines. If the chair bottom was covered with a paper or cloth covering, replace it. Cover all chairs of set in the same manner.

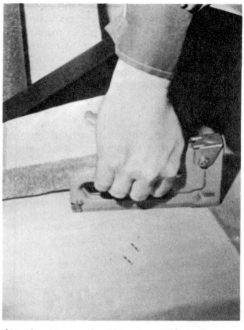

Attach new seating simply with staple gun.

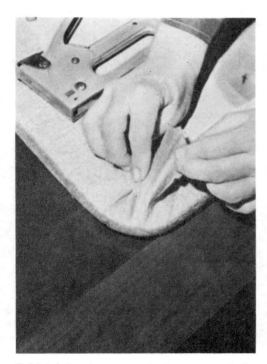

Fold fabric at corners to form smooth fit.

Hammer can be used instead of staple gun.

59

Fixing Cane Seats: The most frequent solution to a broken through cane chair seat is usually a piece of plywood, often upholstered. It is not difficult to replace the cane, however. There are two methods, one involving strands of cane which are woven between holes in the chair frame. The other involves pre-woven cane which is held in grooves or slots by a wedged spline driven in flush.

The pre-woven cane can be purchased at many large hardware stores catering to decorators, or from mail order supply houses. To install first remove the old cane. If it has been woven on the chair itself, the pre-woven cane will not work since it must go into the old grooves. Remove the thin wooden splines from the grooves and rout out the old cane there too. It may have been glued, but it has to come clean.

Place the pre-woven cane over the opening and carefully mark the outside edge of the grooves on it, all around. Cut just a hair, say 1/16" outside this line. Then soak the cane in warm water until soft. While it is soaking, make sure the splines are in good condition. If not, make new ones. Then place the softened cane over the seat so it lines up with the grooves. Coat the splines with white glue and tap one partially in so the edges of the cane are trapped in the groove but not driven tight. Then place the spline in the opposite groove, also trapping the cane ends. Then do the same for the other two sides. When all of the cane ends are trapped in the grooves all around by the splines, they can be driven in. This will pull the cane fairly tight. Take care that there are no wrinkles. Let the cane dry which will shrink it a little tighter. Then plane or sand off the tops of the splines, making them flush. The job's done.

Weaving cane strands on the seat itself is not difficult either, but it does take time and patience. The drawings show how it is done for a perfectly square seat. When the seat is wider at the front, the last couple of front-to-back strands will attach to the side frame holes in order to keep them parallel. The weaving then proceeds as for a square frame. Always start the first strand in the center hole of the front side and go to the center hole of the rear side, working towards both edges. The bitter end is coiled around a strand underneath. The final job can be shellacked, if desired.

Pre-woven cane is purchased by the yard.

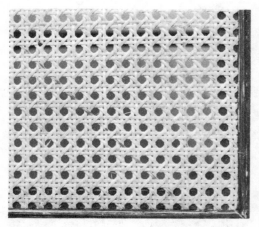

Edges of cane are tapped into grooves.

Rescuing Sick Furniture

Have fun and apply your creativity in forming your own unique chair caning patterns.
Caning is best started in the center of the vertical rows and worked toward the outer edges.
You may choose to follow this popular pattern of subsequent steps to complete seat.

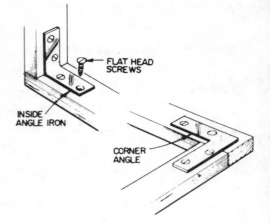

INSIDE ANGLE IRON

FLAT HEAD SCREWS

CORNER ANGLE

The Basics of Upholstery: Step by step instructions for specific chairs must be made on an individual basis to accommodate all the variations. The basics of upholstery, however are common to all styles and can be learned and applied to your particular needs. Upholstered chairs are made up of a wooden frame; a set of metal springs or steel or fabric webbing; some form of padding, cotton batting, horsehair, or foam rubber; and a cloth or leather covering. Turn your chairs over to locate these parts and the attaching points.

If chair's arm or back is loose, the fabric seams covering these joints must be carefully opened and pulled away to expose the wood joints. Re-nailing, re-gluing or the installation of small metal L-brackets for stronger support can correct this problem.

CHAIR CORNER BRACES

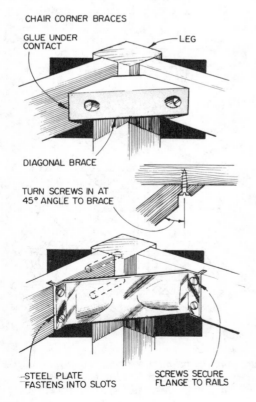

GLUE UNDER CONTACT

LEG

DIAGONAL BRACE

TURN SCREWS IN AT 45° ANGLE TO BRACE

STEEL PLATE FASTENS INTO SLOTS

SCREWS SECURE FLANGE TO RAILS

Chairs that have upholstered backs are unscrewed and covered the same way except the finishing back cover is folded down about ½ inch on all edges and tacked down with matching upholstery nails. The entire back is then re-attached to chair upright. Re-screw seat to the chair piece. After having done this several times the screw holes may become loosened. Fill them with plastic wood and attach screws. They will dry hard and set.

This same procedure can be followed in covering a worn, stained card table or just for decorative effect. After fabric or plastic is neatly tacked in place the tacked edge can be covered with a strip of plastic tape to prevent snags in handling. If more decoration is desired, the sides can be trimmed with colored or metallic upholstery tacks.

Some wood-topped tables can be covered with a self-adhesive paper, which comes in a variety of colors in 18-inch widths and adheres to almost any surface. If using fabric backed plastics for any of these jobs, carefully warm the edges with a medium-hot iron on the fabric side, with a towel to protect it. The warmed plastic softens slightly and makes a smoother edge.

Springs are either coils vertically placed, or no sag type, which is a flat wavy-shaped metal which is tied together or joined by small horizontally placed coils. The spring coils are either nailed to wood cleats at the base of the chair or rivet-fastened to metal webbing, or cord sew-tied to fabric webbing. They are

Rescuing Sick Furniture

tied to each other at the top. This tying is then nailed to the frame. If the top tying has come loose, remove the fabric from the seat area and re-tie the springs following the manner of those still tied. Pull the cord before nailing to re-shape the seat. Then nail the cord to the frame and re-place the fabric.

If the coils have come through on the bottom, the wood cleat may have separated from the frame: re-nail it. Or it may have split: replace it or brace it with a wood or metal strip spanning the split. If the spring is separated from the cleat or metal strip or webbing it needs to be re-nailed, re-riveted or re-tied.

No sag springs are attached to the frame with special metal clips. These may have come loose: re-nail them. The coils connecting the spaces may have popped: hook them back on, twisting the clip end with a pliers for more hookability, or tie these cross springs with heavy cord and nail cord to the frame.

Where padding has become misshapen, carefully remove the fabric covering of that entire area and remove the worn padding. Replace it with new padding of the same type or easier to handle foam rubber sheeting. This can easily be cut with a scissor or sharp exacto knife. Tack or glue this padding to the frame and re-cover the area.

Replacing the fabric covering involves careful separation of existing fabric at all seams, saving pieces to be used as a cutting guide for the new fabric. Save all cording strips to be recovered and re-used. Much of the new fabric can be tacked to the frame. Some parts may have to be machine-sewn, and finished edges will probably need to be blind stitched by hand with curved upholstery needles. This is quite an undertaking for a novice, but not too difficult if taken step by step—and it's a grand accomplishment when completed!

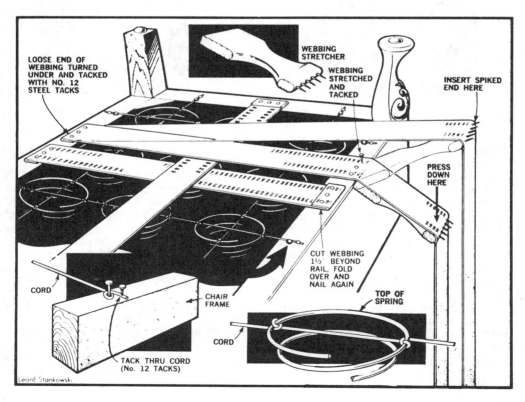

LOOSE END OF WEBBING TURNED UNDER AND TACKED WITH NO. 12 STEEL TACKS

WEBBING STRETCHER

WEBBING STRETCHED AND TACKED

INSERT SPIKED END HERE

PRESS DOWN HERE

CUT WEBBING 1½" BEYOND RAIL, FOLD OVER AND NAIL AGAIN

CORD

CHAIR FRAME

TOP OF SPRING

CORD

TACK THRU CORD (NO. 12 TACKS)

Leone Stankowski

Check for breaks in plastic drawer guide.

Wood strips of side guide must be smooth.

Re-glue any loose dowel joints.

Tie drawer till glue in joints dries.

Drawer Troubles: Crooked-closing drawers can be caused by a misalignment of the center guide. Pull out your drawer and check if it is equipped at the back with a plastic piece that has a holed slot. The dove-tailed center guide of the drawer frame fits into and slides along that slot. It also holds the drawer even when opened. If your drawer tilts forward when it is opened, this piece may be broken. Purchase a new plastic cabinet drawer guide. Unscrew the old and replace it.

Some drawers glide along two-sided wooden protrusions. These can become worn or get frayed with time and weight. If the top face is frayed, remove by prying or unscrewing and reverse top to bottom or right to left, or replace with new wooden strips.

Drawers can become sticky from warping or swelling of the wood. Determine the point of stickiness (you will probably see rub marks on the wood). Sand or plane these areas down and re-test drawer till it rides smooth. If you can't get the drawer out of the desk or dresser, you can dry it by inserting the nozzle of a hair dryer. Let it blow heated air for about an hour—then check if drawer slides.

Drawers may be loosening at corner joints. Do not nail. Nails may split the joint. Re-glue, clamping or tying together with heavy cord until dry.

Drawer pulls sometimes strip and come loose. If wooden, fill with plastic wood, and screw in while wet. Do not pull until dry. See package directions for time needed.

Rescuing Sick Furniture

Flapping Formica: Formica coverings that come loose can be re-glued in the following manner. Carefully lift the formica and insert glue at edges and criss-crossed at center of the area where hold has loosened. Roll down with a rolling pin to smooth and distribute the glue. Place 1x3's with clamps to hold at all edges. Let dry for 24 hours before removing clamps. (If the underside was heavily coated with old glue, you may have to use the vinegar treatment described earlier before re-gluing).

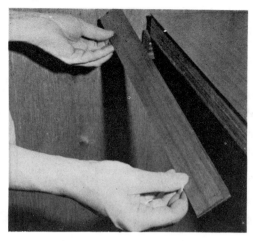

Formica edges often dry and come loose.

Scrape and apply thin coat of adhesive.

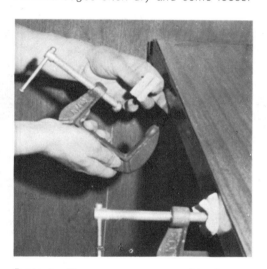

Protect with sponge; secure with clamps.

Loose Bed Slats: Bed slats which support springs are usually just lain into the bed frame, with the springs placed upon them. They can come loose from moving the bed during bed making, or, especially in bunk beds, from being used as a foot rest or pull bar by the person on the bottom. The danger that slats will fall out and all come tumbling down is easily corrected. Place slats at desired location. Drill a hole through the bed frame and slat at that location and insert a roundheaded screw, securing the slat. Do this on all slats, on both sides.

Cabinet Doors That Won't Catch: Cabinet doors often do not close or do not hold closed because of mispositioning of the roller type cabinet catch. There are two adjustable screws which when loosened allow this catch to be moved in either direction, tightening it or loosening it. If the rubber roller has hardened or is paint covered, it needs to be replaced. Other kinds of cabinet catches are a metal prong which fits into a flexible metal groove, or the newer magnetic catches. Any of these install easily with one or two screws.

Patching Veneers: This is one of the simplest repairs to make, and one that can work wonders for the appearance of a desk, table, chair or any piece that is made with a veneer. The veneer is an overlay of fine wood which is glued to the base wood to make the piece more attractive. Since it is only a thin layer, it is frequently chipped.

To make a patch, you must buy a piece of veneer that matches the original's color and grain. Cut the patch large enough to cover the entire damaged area, making it a straight-edged shape such as a triangle or trapezoid.

Place the patch over the broken area and trace around it with a knife. Then carefully cut along that line with a razor and remove the cut section of damaged veneer. Clean the wood underneath, and glue the patch in place. The new piece should be a bit thicker than the surrounding veneer, so when glue is dry, sand patch edges.

If you want to apply a veneer patch to a curved area, wet the patch to make it take the shape. You will have to clamp it in place to make it dry in the desired shape. Then glue in place.

Cut a patch of matching veneer to cover bad spot.

Lay the cut piece over the damaged area and scribe.

Rescuing Sick Furniture

Use razor, steel rule and care to cut away damage.

Test the patch for fit; carefully trim if necessary.

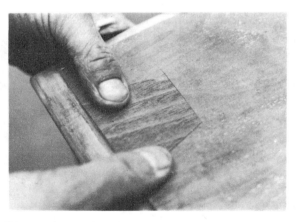

Glue and press patch in place, wiping excess glue.

White Rings or Spots on Wood Surfaces:
These may be caused by moisture, heat, or alcohol from a beverage glass carelessly left on furniture. To remove these most easily, get to work as soon as possible. Stains left to dry and set are more difficult to remove.

Pumice powder or cigarette ash can be applied with 3/0 steel wool, dipped in light oil. Rub lightly, with the grain of the wood. Then lightly go over the entire surface to prevent area shading.

Salt and lightweight oil can be used by dipping your finger into oil, then into salt, and rubbing the mixture into the spot.

Household ammonia will also work. Wet a cloth, wring it out, and moisten it with ammonia. With quick, light strokes, go over the spot. Rub with a dry cloth.

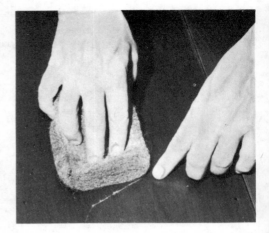

Lightly rub oiled steel wool on scratch.

Covering Scratches: On a natural finish, use a mixture of three parts commercially prepared boiled linseed oil and one part gum turpentine. Heat a small amount of water and place in a small container. Shake the mixture, and pour enough on the heated water to cover the surface. Do not stir. Dip 3/0 steel wool pad into oil layer and lightly rub on scratched surface, moving with the grain. Wipe with a damp cloth; then a dry cloth. Rub at an angle across the scratch with pieces of nutmeats such as walnut, Brazil nut, butternut or pecan until scratch darkens.

On an oil finish, rub scratched area, moving with the grain, with 3/0 steel wool dipped in boiled linseed oil (mineral oil or parafin oil can also be used). Rub entire surface with oil-dampened rag, then with a dry rag.

On a lacquered finish, apply lacquer thinner with small paint brush to blend softened finish over the scratch. When dry rub surface with cloth dipped in rotten-stone and oil.

On a shellac finish, apply shellac thinner or denatured alcohol as above. When dry, rub on entire surface with cloth dipped in pumice and oil.

On a varnish finish apply gum turpentine with a small brush, feathering across the scratch. When dry, rub entire surface with cloth dipped in pumice and oil.

Fill it in with a matching furniture stick.

Gouges, Holes and Burns: Remove the charred area or discolored edge of gouge with 3/0 steel wool wrapped around either the eraser end or the point end of a pencil, depending on the size of the hole. Brush away scrapings. Apply denatured alcohol with a sponge to bleach. If the hole is shallow, or deep and not more than 1 inch wide, fill with sealer or matching lacquer stick. If the hole pierces through to the other side, use spackling compound or plastic wood ' with a lacque dipped into h then feathe to a slight! surface w and carefu dampened dry, smooth necessary.

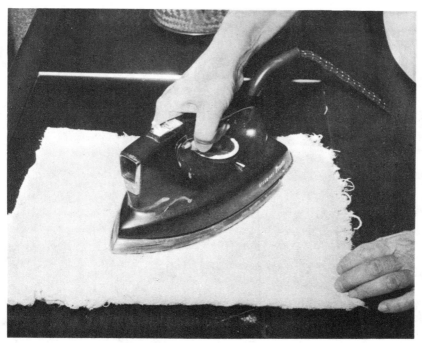

With cloth over the dented area, apply steam from an iron or steamer.

Dents and Bruises: To remove dents and bruises from wood, place a folded cloth or thick woolen blanket over the bruise. Go over the bruised area through the blanket with steam iron. The warm moisture helps wood to swell and resume its previous shape.

Edge and Corner Chips: These can be filled with matching lacquer stick, melted as above. Use a tongue depressor or pop stick and masking tape to frame the corner or form the edge. Fill with melted lacquer. When dry, carefully remove the tape and the sticks. Smooth, if necessary with razor blade and go over with cloth.

Works

orate or repair any kind of wall.

Deco-Wall

With all the beautiful and unusual wall treatments, you can just let your imagination soar.

Types of Walls: A variety of wall constructions can cover the framework creating our walls. It is necessary to know your wall construction in order to know how to attach to it or repair it.

Plastered walls are formed from wood lath strips, or metal lath, or rock lath that is nailed to the studs, to which two or three coats of mortar is applied. The undercoats, a grayish muddy mixture with sand added are called scratch and brown, and the third coat, without sand, is called finish or white.

Hollow wall or dry wall construction is made of sheetrock, a pre-fabricated plaster encased between cardboard sheets, which comes in several thicknesses (½-, ⅝-, ¾-inch) and in 4x8-foot panels or larger sections. These are nailed to the studs. The joints are taped over to form a continuous surface to be painted or papered.

Pre-finished plywood or wood panelling or laminated plastic panelling is either nailed to the studs or glued to a studded frame that has had the addition of horizontal support strips of wood, called furring strips. Or it may be glued or nailed to an existing hollow or plastered wall.

Masonry walls found in some fireproof buildings or exterior walls, are constructed of poured concrete or cinder blocks. These can be painted directly, or papered or panelled.

Behind that decoratively painted, papered or panelled wall is where all the pipes, wires, and ducts are hidden and where what frames and holds up your house, including that decorative wall is found. Wall framing is usually made of 2x4's called *studs* placed vertically approximately 14 inches apart, which makes them 16 inches OC (On Center) with 1 inch to the center of the 2-inch side of each stud. Some localities allow wider spacing to 24 inches OC, and use of 2x3's. They are attached at the bottom to a horizontal 2x4 laid wide side down and anchored to the foundation, and attached at the top in the same way to a top plate. Door and window openings are built into these vertical spaces, and horizontal bracers are sometimes placed between the studs.

We need this basic behind-the-walls knowledge because in attaching or anchoring anything to walls it is best to anchor into a stud. We can find one horizontally at the floor and ceiling line, on all sides of windows and doors, at corners and approximately 16 to 24 inches apart otherwise.

Here is a view inside the average wall, with the names of all of the supporting beams.

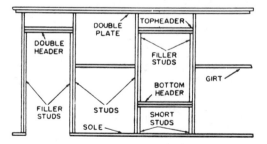

Wall Works

Dressing Up Walls: Decorative walls can be constructed over the sheet rock, plaster or masonry base, giving a finished look that defies its humble beginnings.

Simulated brick or stone finishes require that walls be cleaned and sanded to give a slightly roughened surface. Then apply the *mastic* to a four square foot area. Mastic comes in grey or black and does not set quickly, so that you have time to arrange and re-arrange your patterns. If parts of bricks are needed, just score with a scoring knife and snap to separate. The stone pieces come in many sizes and shapes, so that you can always find a piece to fill in your pattern. Apply

mastic to each brick or stone and set in place with a slight side to side motion. Check and adjust level line of brick. Smooth mastic joints with a wooden stick. Sand corners or butted joints, let dry, and you have a beautiful new wall.

Vinyl brick panels are less real looking but still attractive. They come in 12x20-inch pre-glued pieces which have pre-cut removable tabs for a staggered brick effect. The tabs are to be removed only when joining with another panel. Leave them on at corners and wall edges. Make a level line. Work from top to bottom. Fit each piece with paper backing intact. Cut or trim to space. Remove the paper backing and press into place.

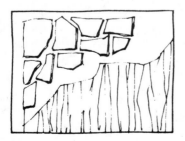
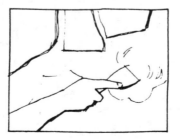
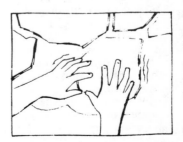

First plan your work, making sure you've got sufficient material. Use broken pieces to fill in smaller spaces. Then, being sure wall is smooth and clean, apply mastic with a putty knife, maintaining ⅟₁₆-inch thickness. Apply a thin layer of mastic to the back of each stone; press.

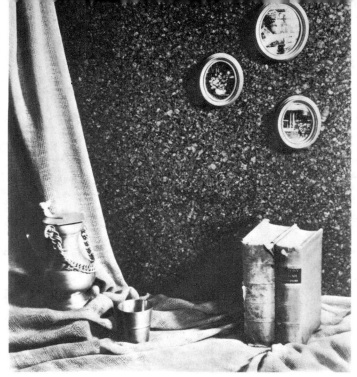

A warm-looking wall of natural cork can be put up in minutes.

Mirror squares are sold in 9- or 12-inch sizes and in clear, gold veined smoked, and designed patterns. They come with double faced foam tape strips. Mark off the area to be mirrored. It should be a multiple of the size mirror you are using to avoid cutting. Smooth any bumpy areas on the wall by sanding. Mark a level and squared line at center of the area to be covered. If you are covering to the ceiling be sure to measure before sticking on any tiles, since the ceiling line may slant or wave. Apply tape strips to mirror corners and stick in place along the squared line. Continue placing squares along level line, keeping the edges even. A wall of mirror tiles goes up in no time and holds securely. If in time you have reason to remove these mirrors, place a thin sharp blade through the center of the foam strip at each corner and cut through strip to remove the mirror. Scrape and sand the rest of the tape from the wall surface.

Cork panels or squares can be installed the same as the mirror squares with two-sided adhesive foam tape, and they make a great wall for bulletins. The bark texture enhances the wall's appearance.

Plan so uncut squares are at wall edges.

Ceramic tile can be cemented onto a lath base or put with adhesive onto a sheetrock wall or any smooth surface. They come in 4-inch squares or 6x9-inch rectangles, or on net backing in varied sizes and patterns. Apply the mastic with a serrated trowel. Place and space your tiles or tile sheet, maintaining a level line. To cut solid tiles, score on back with a glass cutter, place on a sharp counter edge or over a nail and press both ends down. The tile will part on the scored line. For odd shaped cuts around pipe holes, use pliers to nip off small chunks around the desired line, then smooth with a carborundum stone. Varied edge and joint pieces are available for ease of installation.

Let mastic dry for a day. Then soak joints several times before *grouting.* Mix grout to a consistency of heavy cream, and let it stand fifteen minutes; then remix. Apply with a sponge, a window squeegee or by hand. Just smear on, press into all joints, smooth over and groove into joints with a pop stick or tooth brush handle. A damp sponge will clean off the excess grout from the tile surface.

Simulated carved wood squares of Styrofoam can be permanently installed with mastic or put on with the two-sided foam tape. These are great for an accent wall or as an eye catcher on door panels, head boards, cornices, or room dividers.

Perforated hardboard-pegboard has many functional and decorative uses in the workshop, laundry room, kitchen and den, for keeping items stored handily, efficiently and colorfully. A variety of hooks is available. The perforations come in ¼- and ½-inch sizes. To apply it over an existing wall, spacers or furring strips must be used to allow room for hook penetration. It is attached (nailed or screwed) to your particular wall just as any other hang-up.

Recreate the look of Florentine marble . . .

or apply an all-time favorite—neat tiles.

Carved "wood" can be of durable vinyl.

Patching Damaged Walls: For small dents, cracks, or chips in any kind of wall the simplest repair material is *spackle.* It comes in a white powdery form that you mix with water to the consistency of soft toothpaste. Press into cracks with a putty knife and smooth off. Let dry. Sand smooth with fine sandpaper and you're ready to paint over.

If a plastered wall has a larger hole than spackling can help, cut out plaster along the crack or around the hole in an inverted V-shape so the crack is wider inside than at the surface. A beer can opener is a good tool for this job. You may want to drive small nails at regular intervals into the lath, with the heads mid way between surface and lath, to give patching plaster a firmer base. Soak all edges of the opening with water. Fill hole with patching plaster and smooth to ¼ -

inch below the surface with a putty knife or trowel. Allow to partially set, then smooth up to surface line. Let dry fully, then sand smooth. Seal the patch with shellac before painting.

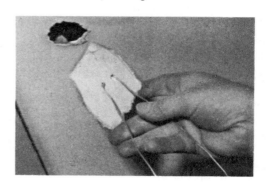

Slip cardboard or screen behind the hole.

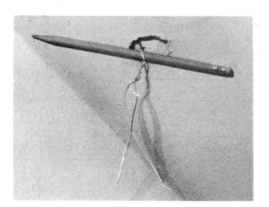

Tie the string to a pencil to hold it taut.

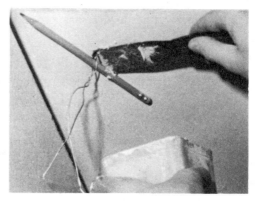

Fill hole half way with patching plaster.

In sheetrock walls or plastered walls where the lath backing is destroyed, chip out the edge of the area to be patched. Knot a piece of string, wire or elastic and thread it through the center of a piece of screen or cardboard which is cut just slightly larger than the hole. Push or slip the screen or cardboard behind the hole, line it up and pull taut by the string. Hold in place, or tie string to a stick that will span the space. Fill the hole to half the thickness of the wall with patching plaster. Score the surface with a nail and let dry. Cut string and fill the hole to surface level. Smooth, let dry, and then sand. Seal with shellac and you're ready to paint.

If the damage is to an even larger area,

a whole panel of sheetrock may need replacing; or you can chisel out to the nearest stud attachment and cut across horizontally above and below break. Cut a piece of sheetrock to fit this space and nail to studs. Tape horizontal joints and nailed joints.

Ceramic tiles sometimes crack from some accidental sharp blow. You should keep extra tiles stored from the original job, as it is difficult to match tiles after a period of time. Pry out the cracked loose tiles and scrape out all old mastic and grout. Sandpaper the area and apply new mastic. Press in the replacement tile. Let dry and re-grout.

About Paints and Painting: Painting is done to create decorative effects, for improvements of sanitary conditions, and to affect the light condition and emotional atmosphere of a room. There are discrepancies in claims from manufacturer to manufacturer regarding what paint is best for where. Trade names and the number and combination of products available add to the confusion; technical chemical terms on labels detailing contents don't help.

To clear the confusion, consider these basic points: the substance to be painted (metal, sheetrock, plaster, wood, concrete, unpainted or previously painted surface); location (exterior or interior); finish desired (flat, semi-gloss, high gloss, textured, rust-proof, washable, waterproof); color (not all kinds and qualities come in specific colors and fashion shades); convenience (coverability in one or two coats, ease of clean-up); price (highest price is not always best, yet the lowest priced is probably lacking some of the qualities of the highest . . . balance your judgement on price against what you're getting with regard to your other considerations).

Our paint chart may help you in making decisions.

A basic distinction between paints is the base. Water-based paints are thinned and the tools used are cleaned with water; an obvious convenience.

Oil-based paints are thinned and tools used are cleaned with turpentine.

Water-based latex paint should not be used directly on top of an oil-based paint, since the oil-water mixture causes an uneven bond and a streaky finish. If you have an oil-based painted surface on which you wish to apply a latex, a primer seal paint must be applied over the old paint first. Latex paint is porous (a breathing paint) and allows moisture to seep out as vapor and so avoids moisture problems. Oil-based paint seals the surface, is non-porous and traps moisture below the surface. If there is a moisture problem in

INTERIOR PAINT SELECTOR

Surfaces	Latex Flat Wall Finish	Latex Satin Gloss Enamel	Satin Eggshell	Dry Swift Enamel & Aerosol	Porch and Floor Enamel	Interior Wood Stains	Latex Flat Wall Enamel
Walls							
Plaster	•	•	•				•
Putty Coat and Sand Finish	•	•	•				•
Wallboard	•	•	•				•
Masonry and Concrete Block	•	•	•				•
Ceilings							
Plaster	•						•
Acoustical	•						•
Masonry	•						•
Trim							
Wood	•	•	•	•		•	•
Metal	•	•	•	•			•
Floors							
Wood					•	•	
Concrete					•		
Miscellaneous							
Wood Paneling						•	
Furniture & Cabinets			•	•		•	

your home or locality this must be considered.

Epoxy paint comes in many decorator colors. It produces a finish that looks like glazed tile; can be applied with a brush or roller or spray gun; has a water resistant quality; bonds to any surface including concrete, tile and porcelain and is great for garage floors, laundry tubs, brick and concrete basement walls, badly crazed tile walls, worn sinks and tubs and appliances. Epoxies come in two components which need to be mixed before applying—follow directions on the can.

Rustproof paints are unique and ideal for metal furniture, outdoor equipment, railings and anywhere that rust presents a problem.

Tools needed for painting are simply brushes and rollers. When buying brushes, consider the size of the area you must cover. The best brushes have three rows of bristles, which should be resilient and should have a chisel edge for sharply defined lines. Rollers are generally used with a paint tray, and come in widths from 9 to 13 inches, with handles of various lengths. A mop stick can be inserted in the handles to do floors, ceilings or tops of walls.

A new, self-feed roller, called the fountain-type, holds up to a pint of paint at a time. The paint oozes through the core to the surface as needed, or is controlled by a trigger action. This offers the convenience of no need for a tray, and no interruption of painting to dip for paint.

Protective measures when painting start with you yourself. Wear gloves and a painter's cap or shower cap. If using sand paint on ceilings, use goggles. For the house and furnishings, be sure to concentrate furnishings in the center of the room and cover with drop cloths. Lightweight plastic sheets are available for the job inexpensively. Use masking tape on window panes, and paint guards at baseboards and cabinet joints.

A great non-tip holder for your can of paint is a large empty detergent box, with a hole cut in one side for the can to be inserted into. This will keep drips off the floor, and will provide a place to rest the brush between uses.

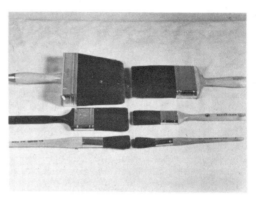

A first-rate job depends on good brushes.

New edge painters work great on moldings.

Smooth out walls before you start to paint.

Edge guides are handy for doing neat work.

Prepare the walls before you paint. Patch all cracks, chips and nail-holes. Scrape, sand and rub with steel wool any area of blistering, loose or peeling paint. The surface must be clean and dust free. If greasy, wash down with grease-removing agent. Wash from the bottom up, to avoid streaks. Shellac over any bad stains that might bleed through; brush over with a coat of spackle.

If you choose to paint over a wallpapered surface, removal of the paper is quick and easy with chemical wallpaper removers. In some instances, paper can be painted over. Test a small area for bleeding, coverability and texture.

Painting tips. Primer base coats are necessary on all new surfaces. A combination of brush and roller is best for most jobs. Use the brush at corners of ceiling, on wood trim, and on windows and doors. This is called "cutting in." Do this on each wall, then follow up with the roller on all flat surfaces.

Apply paint only with the end of the bristle, turning brush often. Lift brush gradually ending in a "feather" stroke so as not to leave thick edges of paint. Always try to paint full areas at one time. Paint with the grain of the wood. Except for overhead work do not paint with bristles up.

Red Devil Paint

Or clean-up edges on glass with a scraper.

For roller painting, coating the tray with aluminum foil aids in clean-up or quick color change. Fill the tray only half way to avoid slop-over. Roll down the tray slope to get paint on the roller and then roll back up the slope to distribute the paint evenly and drain off excess. Do not bear down on the up-stroke so much as to squeeze out all the paint, but don't bring it out splashing and dripping. When applying to the wall don't apply strong pressure on first strokes; just enough to make it roll instead of sliding. Then as the roller is less full, apply stronger pressure to ease out as much paint as you can before re-dipping. Recommended strokes are V- or W-shaped, then fill in to get initial paint spread to a wider area. Keep the roller motion angular, so that the whole area is covered by rolling motion, not by starts and stops, pick-ups, or sidewise smearing or spinning. The main consideration is to get an even coat.

Clean-ups with water-base paints should be done as soon as you are finished; wash everything out with plain water. For oil base, do it with turpentine. While the paint is still wet on brushes, rollers and pans this is an easy, quick job, but after it dries it is messy, time consuming, and wasteful of good equipment. After a good clean-up on brushes, run an old brush, comb or table fork through the bristles to straighten them, then wrap in freezer paper or aluminum foil. Fold, squaring off the edge and covering up to the handle. For storage hang from a hole in the handle or lay flat. Never stand brush on its bristles. Neglected brushes worth saving could be reclaimed by cleaning with liquid brush cleaner or paint and varnish remover.

Seal can covers tightly on leftover paint. If lumps or skin form, paint should be strained through a mesh screen or cheesecloth before re-use.

Paper and Paperhanging: The special items you'll need for this are a paste pail, paste brush, wallpaper brush, seam roller, sponge, single-edged razor blade or trimming knife, yardstick, scissors and a good size worktable.

Wall preparation for papering is the same as described for painting.

How much paper you need is deter-mined by the length of each wall to be covered, the height of the ceiling, and the dimensions of doorways or windows. The paper dealer will be able to determine how many rolls you need. It's a good idea to buy one extra roll with the guarantee that it is returnable if not opened. The dealer will also give you the correct paste for the kind of paper you choose. Also, ask him about sizing, which is a wall preparation required by some pastes.

Patterns will coincide on each paper roll.

To put up the paper, start by preparing your paste, as it will have to set a short while before applying. Set up your worktable. Then, start at an inconspicuous corner, which draperies or furniture will cover, since the last joint of the pattern is likely not to match exactly. Determine the vertical line of this corner with a plumb bob (a lead weight at the end of a long string which indicates true vertical line), or a level or T square.

Cut a strip of paper the length from your ceiling to your baseboard with about 1½ inch extra at either end to accommodate for sloping baseboards and ceilings. Now measure off a second piece, matching the pattern, and cut. Some paper hangers continue this process and cut all the strips at one time. I prefer to measure just one strip ahead to avoid confusion, and so that in the possibility of a measuring goof you're only out one strip (which can be used for over doors and under windows, etc.).

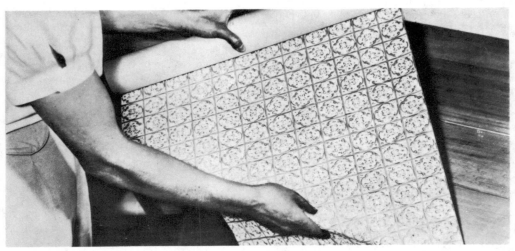

1. If the wallpaper comes too tightly rolled, straighten it out along the edge of a table.

3. Brush paste on half of the paper and fold over to center. Then repeat on other half.

Wall Works

Lay your first strip, pattern side down, on your table and brush on the paste to mid way. Fold over top half of paper resting paste on paste, and keeping a rounded fold. Apply paste to balance of strip, folding in the same manner. Now carry this piece to your starting corner being sure you have it right side up. Unpeel the top from its paste fold and apply at ceiling line. Line up side with vertical line or corner, brushing from the center of the strip to either side to smooth. Unpeel bottom half lining up and smoothing in same fashion. Brush tightly into ceiling and baseboard and trim with razor or trimming knife. Wipe any excess glue on paper with moistened sponge.

Now cut the third strip, matching the pattern to the second, and lay aside. Paste second strip on as the first, and apply to wall in same manner, butting the joint. Trim at top and bottom, then smooth butted seam joint with seam roller.

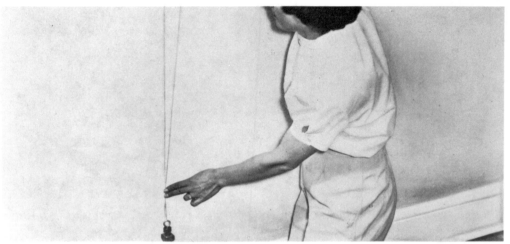

2. *Use a plumb bob to snap a line of chalk on the wall. This indicates the true vertical.*

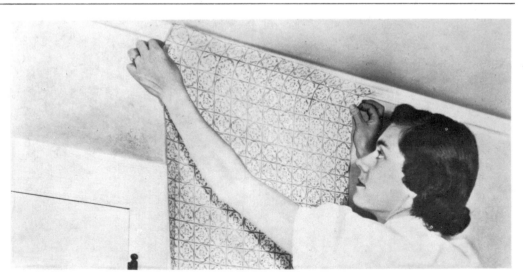

4. *Apply the paper to the wall, being sure to line up edge with the vertical line marked.*

(Continued on next page)

When reaching a door or window that has a wood trim frame, stiffly corner paper with brush into the vertical wood frame and trim with razor. Cut paper horizontally at window or door top and bottom and continue to spread paper full width.

When covering areas with light switches or outlets, shut off electricity, remove plate cover, place on strip of wallpaper then trim at the edge of the outlet hole and re-attach plate.

When reaching corners, if a piece extends around the corner, push tightly into corner with the brush, slit at corner line

5. Pull down bottom of paper; brush flat.

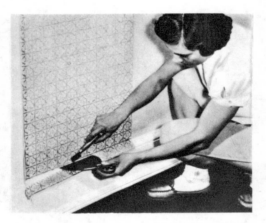

6. Brush firmly at the ends and razor-trim.

9. Smooth butted seam joint with a roller.

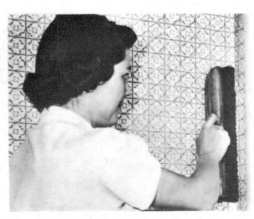

10. Brush paper tightly in corners; slit.

and wipe down with sponge. If the piece ends exactly at the corner, allow the new piece to overlap ¼ inch. When reaching the last corner, allow to overlap.

Small air bubbles that persist under the paper can be pierced with a pin. If somehow a blob of paste or slight recession in the wall makes for uneven fit, a careful slit with the razor blade and a smoothing over with the sponge will correct the fit and hardly be noticeable. Any edges that curl may need a bit more paste, which can be applied with a finger, and then re-rolled with seam edger.

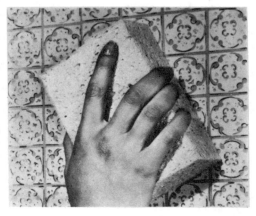

7. Wipe excess glue with moistened sponge.

8. Line up second strip; match the print.

11. Remove all outlet plates; paper; trim.

12. Apply self-stick paper in similar way.

Fabric Wall Coverings: Using fabric on walls is an easy way to create exciting rooms. Aside from the color and texture fabrics add, they can also be great coordinators in a room. For instance, you can match the wallcovering to a bedspread or to pillows, or match it to a set of curtains trimmed with the fabric. The possibilities are almost endless.

And now, you don't even need to bother with the equipment and time involved in wallpapering to put up a wall of fabric. It can be done with a staple gun, or with double face tape. Either one will eliminate the problems of air pockets, wrinkles and uneven joints.

If using tape, first, make sure that the wall surface is free of dust and dirt, or else the tape won't hold securely. Turn under edges of fabric and stitch down, or glue with white glue. Then just put the tape on the fabric, then press the fabric on the wall.

Generally, the smoother the wall the easier it will be to put up fabric, so that brick or textured panels may be tricky.

Avoid using very heavy fabrics. For moderately heavy fabrics, use an extra strip of tape down the middle of each fabric panel.

Fabric on wall can match your upholstery.

Apply double face tape along fabric edge.

Remove backing from tape and press firmly.

Here are just a few ideas for ways to dress-up a room by using wallpaper, fabric, and self-adhesive plastic paper. If you've got a knack for sewing, make matching pillows.

Hang-Ups: Lightweight objects can be hung on any wall with nail hooks, picture hooks, adhesive cloth hooks, magic mounts, self stick hooks, double-sided foam tape, staple gun (if it's a penetrable item) thumb tacks, etc. Hanging heavier items requires special anchors and that's where our wall knowledge comes in.

Anchoring into a stud is the best way to hang anything heavy. (Studs are those 2x4's we spoke about under basic wall construction.) Studs at corners and around windows and door frames are found rather easily. Those in the wall, which may vary in their distance apart, are a little harder to find. For hollow wall construction there is a device called a stud finder which you slide along the wall —when a stud is located the arrows hold a fixed position. Actually this works on the principle of a magnet and what it locates is the metal of a nailed joint. It can be helpful, but other metals behind the wall could activate it and deceive you.

Another method for locating a stud is to start from the nearest corner and approximate a 16- to 24-inch space and tap on the wall. In the non-studded area you would hear a hollow sound. When you reach a stud you hear a solid sound. When you locate the necessary studs, drill the appropriate size holes, and insert screws for attaching your bracket or whatever.

To hang a large mirror or weight-bearing shelves or modular furniture, you should not depend on wall anchors (discussed later) but must connect the piece to studs. If the stud location is not in line with the attaching point of your mirror or bracket, get one or several finished pieces of 1x4-inch wood, equal in length to the piece you intend to hang. This will span two or more studs. Measure off your piece and nail the board into the studs within this measurement to hold it in place. Then drill and screw the board into the studs with screws long enough to penetrate 1 inch into the stud. Finish the piece to match the wall if you choose a finished look. Then nail or screw your shelf bracket, mirror hook or cabinet mount into this 1x4 for a sturdy attachment.

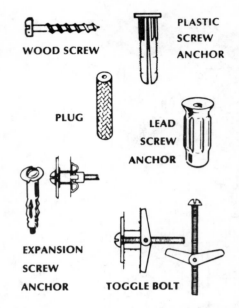

WOOD SCREW

PLASTIC SCREW ANCHOR

PLUG

LEAD SCREW ANCHOR

EXPANSION SCREW ANCHOR

TOGGLE BOLT

For plastered walls fibre plugs and plastic or lead anchors are recommended. A hole just big enough to admit the anchor, and slightly smaller than the plug, is drilled into the wall. The anchor or plug is tapped into the hole. Your item is screwed into the anchor or plug, which spreads inside the wall forming a tight anchor.

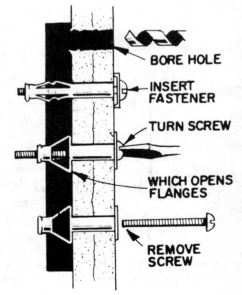

BORE HOLE

INSERT FASTENER

TURN SCREW

WHICH OPENS FLANGES

REMOVE SCREW

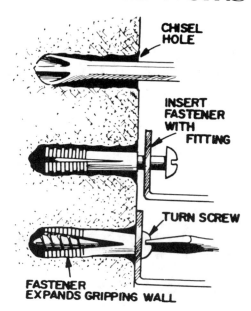

For masonry walls, steel cut nails or concrete nails can be used. Adhesive nails, which look like nails with large square perforated heads, can be secured to masonry with a blob of special adhesive. Boards then can be driven onto the protruding nail. The nail is then clinched (protruding end is bent flat). For attaching other kinds of brackets to masonry use a lead, fibre or plastic shield. A hole must be drilled into the masonry with a special carbide tipped masonry bit or a star drill and hammer. The shield is inserted into the hole and a lag screw is inserted through your item and into the shield. As it screws in, it spreads the shield against the masonry wall for a tight anchor.

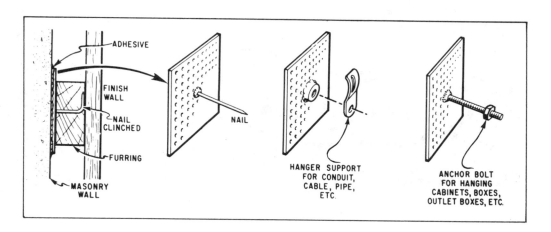

For hollow walls, molly fasteners and toggle bolts are recommended. I find toggle bolts to be more reliable. They have a wing-type attachment. A hole must be drilled large enough to admit the folded wing. Since the hole to admit the wing is larger than the bolt, it makes a tighter fit if you place a bushing or wood spacer on the shank of the bolt between the bracket and the wing before inserting. Insert the bolt through your bracket and through the bushing, then thread on the wing and, with it folded towards you; insert it into the hole and tighten the bolt. If several are being used, as on an upright bracket, none can be tightened until all are inserted. When the wing is inserted it opens behind the wall and as the bolt is tightened it grips the wall for a tight anchor. Once they are in they are not retrievable. Unscrewing the bolt will cause the wing to fall behind the wall.

Doors and Windows
Keeping them in shape and dressing them up.

Lovely to look at, doors and windows are also vital to the functioning of your home.

Doors are classified by the way they are attached to the frame (hinged or track), the method of opening (swinging, folding, gliding), and their construction (solid, hollow, paneled, glass-paned, louvre, etc.).

Exterior and apartment entrance doors are hinged, bear locks and latches, and are fitted into squared-off frames.

Troubles with Hinges: Hinges are two part metal plate assemblies with staggered-spaced barrel shafts which fit together and are held together by a removable pin. The pin slips into the joined barrel shaft, and can be removed by tapping upon the barrel head. It slides out and the hinge parts separate.

Squeaky Doors: These can be corrected by squirting a little oil, graphite or silicone lubricant into the hinge pin area. Work the lubricant in by swinging the door several times.

Sometimes one or both hinges are too tightly placed, or uneven. Check the square of the door (you can use a level for this). If it tilts out on top, remove the lower hinge from the jamb side and insert a piece of cardboard the same size as the hinge plate to act as a shim (a leveling device). Re-attach door and check for better square. If the door skews out at the bottom do the same to the top hinge.

If the door is square but both hinges are too tight, the barrel isn't free of the jamb, so shim both hinges. The shimming of the hinges may then necessitate the sanding or planing of the door on the latch side.

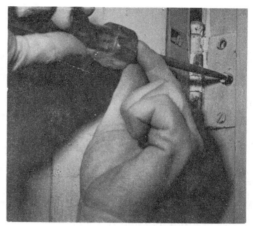

Remove hinges by taking out holding screws.

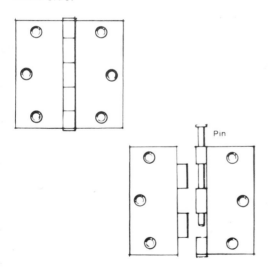

Swing type doors operate on basic hinges, made of two metal plates joined by a pin.

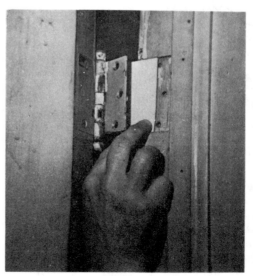

Hinge can be built up by inserting a shim.

A Tight Fit: Hinge troubles may cause trouble with the fit, so again, check these first. Determine the location of the rubbing sticking or swelling. Mark off. With door closed, remove the hinge pin by placing the screwdriver directly under the head of the pin and tapping with a hammer in an upward direction. You will note the pin starts to rise. Continue tapping until the pin lifts out. Repeat same on lower pin. (If the pin does not give easily it may be overcrusted with many layers of paint. Chip away the old paint or brush on paint remover. Allow working time, then remove easily.) Open the door and separate from the hinge section. Lay door on one end and plane down to the marked area.

With installation of carpeting, the bottom of the door may not be able to close. This may be more than a planing job, and you will have to saw the needed amount off.

Replace the door by aligning the hinge barrel and re-inserting the hinge pin. Check for fit. You may have to repeat the operation to get door working well.

Remove doors by tapping up on hinge pin.

A Too Loose Fit: This is caused by shrinkage of the wood or installation of an improper size door. The door may rattle and the latch may not reach the strike plate and therefore not hold closed. To correct this, unscrew the hinges from the jamb. Place cardboard strips the same size as the hinge leaf under the hinge and re-attach. This should tighten the door and force it closer to the latch side so it can catch.

If this is not enough to correct the situation, remove the strike plate. Get a thin strip of wood the full length of the jamb and nail or screw in place on the latch side (or just build up the strike plate area). Chisel out the hole for the bolt and the flush mount of the strike plate and re-attach the strike plate.

If lock becomes loose and screws holding face plate are visible; tighten them here.

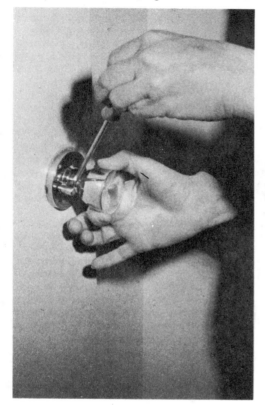

RECESSING A HINGE

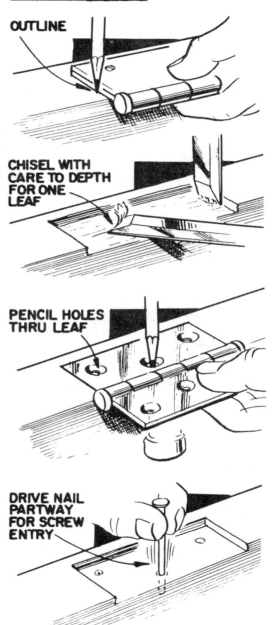

OUTLINE

CHISEL WITH CARE TO DEPTH FOR ONE LEAF

PENCIL HOLES THRU LEAF

DRIVE NAIL PARTWAY FOR SCREW ENTRY

Depending on how ill a fit you have, you might have to add a strip like this to the hinge side of the door. Remove the door and take off the hinges. Nail on the needed strip. Groove out the space for recessing of the hinge, as shown in the diagrams, and re-hang the door. Paint or finish the strips to match your door frame. **A Loose Doorknob:** If the screws are visible on the outer rim, just tighten them. If the screws are not visible, remove the knob and rim from the inside (see instructions for *Replacing a Door Lock*). Screws will then be visible. Tighten them. Replace rim and knob.

Hinges must be set in so they are flush with side of door and so the pin clears.

Troubles with the Latch Catch: Hinge troubles may cause troubles with the latch catch, so check hinges first.

The strike plate is that metal piece with a square hole in it that is attached to the frame on the open side. The bolt is the part of the latch that fits into the hole and keeps the door closed. Settling of the house may cause the bolt and the hole not to meet properly, thereby not holding the door closed. To correct this, close door slowly to determine whether the ill fit is at the top or the bottom of the hole. Unscrew and remove the strike plate. If the ill fit is slight enough to be corrected by filing the hole, do so. If it requires more adjustment, mark on the jamb (where you took the strike plate off) where the bolt hits. Place the strike plate, aligning the hole with this mark. Now mark off its raised or lowered line. Chisel out jamb where necessary to fit this line, and to make the strike plate fit flush. Re-attach the strike plate. If the old screw holes overlap and don't allow the screws to grab and hold, plug them with wooden matchsticks, toothpicks or plastic wood.

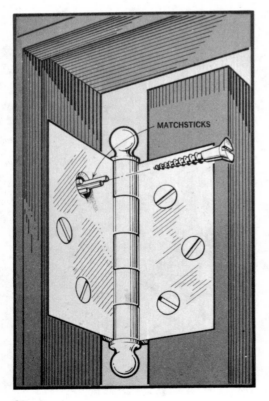

MATCHSTICKS

About Locks: While browsing in your local hardware store, note the types of locks available. For doors alone there are several. 1) An entrance lock is keyed on one or both sides and locks by either a snap button, a push button or a turn piece on the other side. 2) A privacy lock for bathrooms or bedrooms is non-keyed, but locks on one side by a snap button, a push button or a turn piece. An emergency flat bar key, which fits into a small hole on the rim, is included for accidental lock-ins. This key, when inserted into the hole and twisted, releases the lock. 3) Other general knob and latch sets are non-keyed and non-locking. They are called passage knob sets.

There are two types of latch closures, a spring type and a dead bolt. The spring type is beveled at one end and springs in when reaching the strike plate and out when it fits into the bolt hole or is opened. The dead bolt is blunt cut and has only two positions; opened or closed. It cannot be moved from these positions except by hand or key turning of the release knob.

Cylinder locks use keys which raise a series of pins. When all are properly raised, they release the plug, which allows the key to be turned.

Tumble locks utilize a set of seven notches of varying depths on a circular key hole. These are considered among the most pick-proof kind you can get.

There are also surface bolt guards which have a slide bolt that fits into a barrel on the jamb side. One comes with a key for doors with thin panels or glass panes, so that even if the glass is broken the door cannot be opened without a key. These, like the chain guard are simply screwed to the door surface, one piece on the door frame and one piece on the jamb frame, being careful to line up pieces evenly. But with extreme force these can be ripped off.

There is another kind, which is stronger and which is placed *into* the door and bolted inside the jamb. It should come with full details of installation.

Doors and Windows

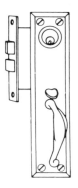 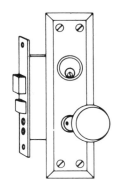

Mortised dead bolt lock can be combined with latch and knob assembly in one unit.

Face plate prevents prying-off of the lock.

Ideal Security

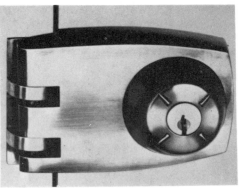

Dead bolt lock can be worked by turn knob.

Dead bolts can be key locked from inside.

Stanley Hardware

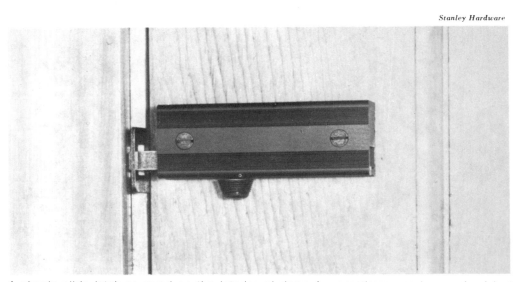

A simple slide latch screwed on the interior of doors is sometimes used as a dead bolt.

Installation of a Look Out Guard: A look out guard, or peep-hole, is a small tubular device with a wide angle lens that allows the person inside to see the person outside without opening the door. Some are one-way viewers, and some have a hinged metal cover to keep outsiders from viewing inside. Either is easily installed by drilling a hole with an expansion bit (a drilling piece with an adjustable cutting arm) or the circular saw attachment of the electric drill. Insert the barrel from the outside and insert the inner viewing piece from the inside. Screw down the frame on the inside, and look out.

Installing Chain Locks: Several chain locks are available which also allow you to see the caller and accept small packages without fully opening the door. One kind has a key so that you can keep the chain on when you are out. In apartments where entry keys might be in several service hands, this is an additional protection. It can, however, be ripped off with extreme force. One part of this is simply screwed to the door frame and one part to the jamb section. The attached chain is slipped into the slide hole.

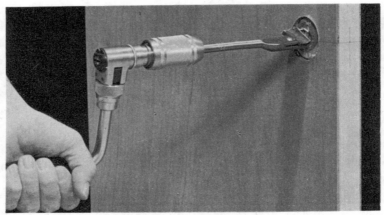

Use expansion brace bit to drill holes for locks and door viewers.

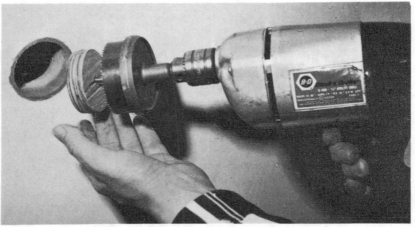

Make holes for locks with a circular saw attachment to electric drill.

Window Locks: The standard type wooden window lock is a two-piece unit in which one piece turns under the groove of the other to lock and turns free to allow opening. There is the possibility that this kind could be pried from the exterior so several kinds have been adapted with bolt turning heads and with key locks, that are usable for sliding aluminum windows also. They all simply install with four screws.

The Lock Is Frozen: This could happen to exterior doors or car doors from extreme cold, wet weather. Dip the key in alcohol or warm it with a match or a cigarette lighter. Insert the key and open. Prevent future trouble by squirting windshield defroster into the lock opening.

Sticky Lock or Rough Key Insertion: The lock mechanism may be dirty. Blow it out with a syringe-type blower or bicycle pump. Spray in powdered graphite or silicone spray lubricant, or rub the key grooves with a lead pencil tip. *Do not* use lubricating oil on locks.

Keyed locks are made for sliding windows.

A chain guard lock screwed on inside of door allows contact with partial door opening.

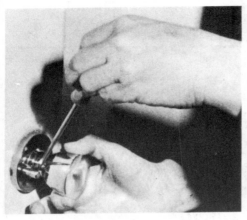

1. Release lock knob by pressing in slot.

2. Knob slides off uncovering face plate.

Replacing a Door Lock: Some locks have two screws on the circular collar around the knob. Remove them and both knobs will be easily pulled out. Other locks have a recessed pushbutton in the shank which you can release with pressure of a screwdriver or nail to remove the inner knob. Pry off the circular plate. Then you will see two screws holding the rest of the mechanism. Remove them and the two knobs will separate and come out. If the latch mechanism is not malfunctioning and you purchase the same type of knob, it is not necessary to remove it. If you must remove the latch, it is easily done by turning the two screws holding it in place.

The new lock is inserted and assembled the same way in reverse order. Install the latch assembly. Insert the outer knob, catching the inner part of the latch assembly. Test to see it activates the latch. Then slide the inner mechanism, lining it up with the screw holes in the outer section, and tighten. Insert the inner cover plate and snap on the knob. Spray with silicone lubricant and test.

New locks come with a template or paper pattern. If you have to install the lock on a new door which has no holes drilled, the pattern is pre-measured and marks off exactly where to drill the proper sized holes to admit the lock and latch assembly.

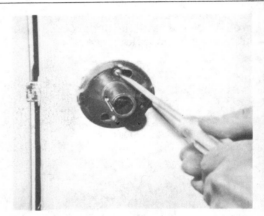

5. Loosen screws; turn plate to release.

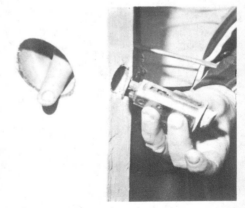

8. If necessary remove latch mechanism.

Doors and Windows

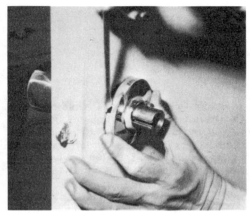

3. Face plate pries off easily with blade.

4. With plate off lock screws are visible.

6. Inner assembly is free and slides off.

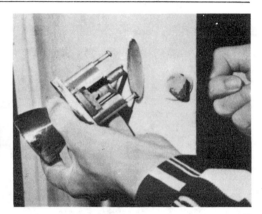

7. Outer assembly is free and slides off.

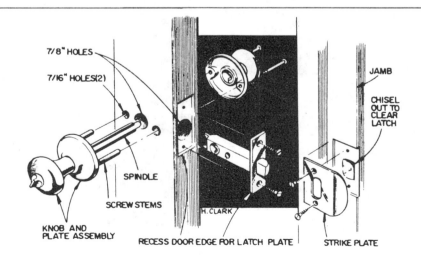

7/8" HOLES

7/16" HOLES(2)

JAMB

CHISEL OUT TO CLEAR LATCH

SPINDLE

SCREW STEMS

H. CLARK

KNOB AND PLATE ASSEMBLY

RECESS DOOR EDGE FOR LATCH PLATE

STRIKE PLATE

Key Is Broken in the Lock: Try to turn or remove it with a pair of pliers. If not enough of the key protrudes to grab, moistened chewing gum usually works. If these don't and you can get inside the lock, remove the cylinder (see *Replacing a Door Lock*), and push the key out with a hat pin.

Key Turns But Does Not Release Lock: The locking mechanism is either dirty, in need of lubricating or damaged. If cleaning and lubricating don't help, replace the lock.

Prevention of Entry by Celluloid Strip: Most beveled spring latches can be easily opened by insertion of a celluloid strip (much like a credit card), which presses in the latch and opens the door. Try it on yours. To foil such illegal entry: 1) Pry up the outside strip of the strike plate, so that the celluloid strip cannot pass, or 2) place two flat-head screws just in front of the strike plate, protruding slightly, so they would catch the strip before it reaches the beveled part of the latch.

Pry up latch plate front to prevent entry.

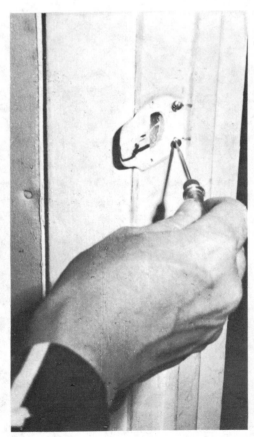

Place two screws in front of latch plate.

Working and Non-Working of a Sliding Door: A metal dual or multiple track is attached to the upper portion of the frame, usually of a closet space. Nylon rollers on hangers attach to the top of each door and ride in one of the tracks. A floor guide keeps the doors moving steadily and prevents swinging in and out. Roller hangers are adjusted by loosening two screws and then raising, lowering or centering, right or left, to get a good fit with the vertical frame. A top mold trim usually covers and conceals this attachment.

The bottom glide fit may become tight from swelling, or it may sag. If it cannot be adjusted at the top, the door may have to be sanded or planed at the bottom. Unscrew the floor guide. Pull the door towards you and unhook the roller from the track. Plane door as much as necessary and replace by hooking onto the track and re-attaching the floor guide.

Weather Stripping and Caulking: Every window and door that opens is a potential area for drafts. In the interest of fuel economy and draft-free comfort, weather stripping of doors and windows is recommended. There are several kinds available on the market, with varying ease of installation. There are metal strips, felt strips, vinyl strips, rubber strips etc., most of which have to be tack nailed. There is a window weather strip that looks like rope and molds like clay, pressing into place with finger tips. It is self adhering, yet removes cleanly and never hardens. It can be used for caulking on the outside also. There is also a closed cell vinyl foam tape that is air tight, water tight, non-absorbing, and which can be applied to windows, doors and air conditioners. It is self adhering and comes in five widths. Place this around the entire frame of the door, except the bottom, at the point where the closed door meets the frame. Door bottoms require a separate piece that screws in place on the inside of the door and has a flexible rubber flap to accommodate opening. The foam or clay type can be pressed on at the joint of the window frame and the window.

Some windows are so drafty as to require the placement of large plastic sheets called plastic storm windows. They are taped down over the entire window frame or onto the wall area. This prevents the opening of the window until it is removed, but it helps keep the drafts out.

Sliding doors can have tracks at top and bottom; screw track into closet heading.

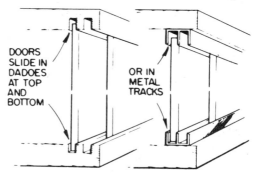

New press-on type caulking applies easily.

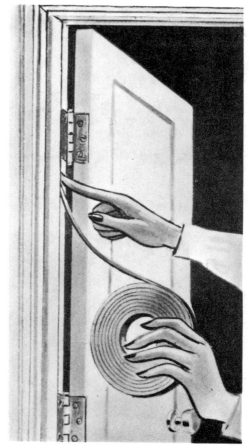

Repairing a Screen: Fiberglass screen cloth can be repaired with a warm iron. Cut a clean square around the damaged part. Cut a patch piece just slightly larger than this hole. Place it over the space; then place a sheet of paper over both of them, being careful not to move the patch piece. Apply the warm iron over the paper. The heat will seal the patch in place.

For metal screening, cut a clean square around the damaged part. Cut a patch piece ½ inch larger on all four sides. Pull out two or three wires from each side leaving a hair-like edge of wires. On a flat-edged block of wood with a spatula or mallet, square off this hair edge, forming right angles. Slip this bent, protruding edge through the squared edges of the damaged area. With mallet or straight edge, bend the hair edge flat on opposite side, using the wood block as backing.

If a whole section of a wooden screen is to be replaced, remove the molding holding the screen in place by prying carefully so as not to split it. Cut the new piece of screening to overlap on frame twice the width of the molding. Fold these edges so that the tacking is through a double layer of screening. Staple or tack in place. A strip of glue under the length of molding before re-nailing helps bond the screening. Corners of wood screens that are loosened can be held firm by screwing flat L-brackets at the corners of the frame.

Some aluminum screen frames separate by removing small screws at the corner joints. Screening is held in the groove by a rubber stripping. Pull this out and remove the torn screening. Replace with new screening. Tap it into the groove with the rubber strip by using a block of wood and a hammer. Trim away any excess screening. Tighten corner screws and re-hang.

Cut a screening patch to fit around hole.

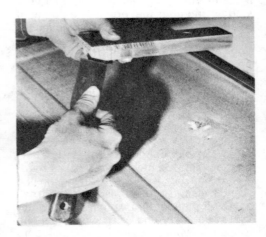

Pull threads from sides; bend over block.

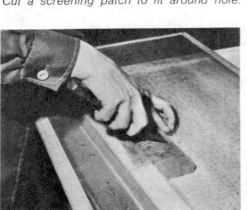

Press bent threads over on opposite side.

Complete patch by smoothing edges down.

GLAZIERS POINTS

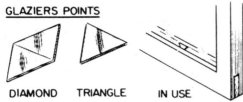

DIAMOND   TRIANGLE   IN USE

Replacing a Glass Pane: With work gloves, carefully remove all broken glass and pry off molding. Carefully chisel out all dried putty. Measure your frame edge to edge and purchase new glass cut to 1/8 inch less on each side. Brush the frame with linseed oil, and line the edge with a bed of putty. Place in the glass piece; edge with a border of putty. Carefully re-nail molding. If there was no molding, drive in glaziers points (triangular nails), two to each side, or one every 6 inches. Cover all edges with a smooth pressed-in line of putty, beveled to fit into corner. After seven to ten days, paint putty to match window. For interior French doors you can replace pane with colored or designed plexi-glass for a decorative effect.

That Rusty Casement Window: Scrape away all loose flaky rust and paint. With hand, wire brush or wire brush attachment to an electric drill, clean down past the rust level on all parts. Vacuum away all dirt from tracks or joints. Oil or spray with silicone all moving parts. Repaint metal frame with damp-proof primer, and then a coat of rust-proof finish color.

① REMOVE BROKEN GLASS, SCRAPE FRAME CLEAN.

② MEASURE OPENING ALLOW 1/8" ALL AROUND.

③ PAINT WITH LINSEED OIL. APPLY THIN COAT OF PUTTY FOR THE SEAL OR BED FOR GLASS

④ SET GLASS AND SECURE WITH GLAZIER'S POINTS

⑤ APPLY PUTTY & SMOOTH TO NEAT EVEN BEVEL

PUTTY KNIFE
PUTTY BED
GLASS
PUTTY

HOW PROPER BEVEL IS OBTAINED

Hollow Doors that Come Away from the Frame: Hollow doors are constructed of a wooden frame with a sheet of masonite or thin wood panelling glued to each side. Sometimes the drying effects of home heating cause the glued panels to loosen and come away from the frame. When this happens on the hinged side, it prevents the door from closing. Remove the door by taking out the hinge pin. Apply glue to the front and back frame on all sides and clamp panelling to the frame with 1x4's to hold it in place until dry. Sand or plane door slightly, as tight fit may have added to the cause for the pulling away. Replace the door and the hinge pins.

Attaching Things to Doors: If the door is panelled or paned and you wish to make it flush (flat-sided), measure the size of the door and get two pieces of masonite hardboard that size. They come in 4x8-foot sheets, but the lumber yard will cut to your size or may have odd pieces around so that you won't have to buy two whole sheets. Remove the door from the hinge. Remove the knobs and any hardware. Apply glue to all edges and panel strips. Place masonite pieces on the door and clamp in place with 1x4's. Let dry. Sand or plane at edges for a clean fit. Cut out knob holes with a circular saw attachment to the electric drill. Replace knobs and replace door in the hinge.

If the fit into the frame is too tight to close, remove hinges from the door and the jamb and move back about 3/16 inch on each. If the old screw holes are effected, fill in with match sticks, toothpicks or plastic wood. Paint or decorate the door to match your room.

Pegboard can be screwed to just the panelled area. The space between the panels would allow hook clearance. Since the pegboard will not cover the part of the door that fits into the frame or knob area, no other adjustment is necessary.

To attach a mirror to a flush door, mark the door with a line at the top and bottom of where you want the mirror to be. Be sure mirror will be centered and level. Screw in two spaced mirror clips a hair below the bottom line, facing up, and two clips a hair above the top line, facing sideways. Place in the mirror and turn the top clips down to hold it. Screw in two spaced mirror clips at each side. Mirror, mirror on the door—who's unhandy anymore?

Hanging racks in hollow doors can be done in the same way as hang-ups for hollow walls (see section on *Walls*). If the racks will bear little weight, screwing them into the door may work, but it's not as secure. If the door is solid wood, racks will hold fine with just screws. For panelled doors, your rack will have to be attached to the thicker wood frames, or be hung from strips of wood that you attach to the frames.

MOLLY HOOK FOR HANGING FRAMES

USE OF JACK-NUT TO SECURE MIRROR TO FLUSH DOOR

Install metal towel rack on back of door.

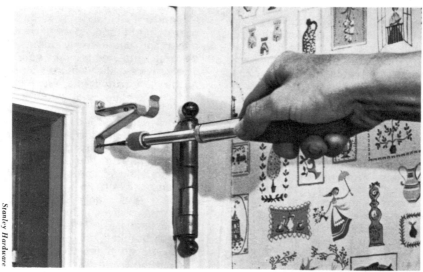

On glass panelled doors, hooks can only be screwed into wooden frame.

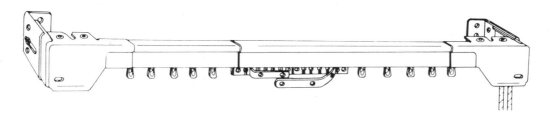

About Curtain Rods: All curtain rods should be screwed in, not nailed. For those bearing any weight and length, special anchors should be used if no stud is located. The basic installation is that of any bracket; drill the hole, and insert the anchor through the bracket into the wall. Much of the trick is in proper measurement, location, spacing, levelling, and choice of rod.

For curtains with a casing and valances, the stationary curtain rod is used. It slips into a metal bracket that screws on the face or inside of the frame.

Tier curtains or draperies to be used with rings need a café rod which rests on a equi-distant protruding brackets.

Draperies on rings that you wish to open, need a traverse café.

Draperies that draw opened and closed and cover the rod use a traverse rod. Many combinations and shapes are available but the bracket installation is all the same; a matter of two or three screws or anchors. The decision on where to place the brackets (on the ceiling, on the wall near the ceiling, at window level, etc.) depends on taste and style.

Traverse Troubles: Minor difficulties are sometimes experienced with traverse rods. The cord may stretch or loosen. If the cord is not taut, you will not get even draw of the drape. Pull the cord so that the drape is fully closed. Locate the knot under the overlap carrier. Pull any extra give and re-knot. Test for easier flow.

If extra glides are left between pleats they tend to sway and jam. Any extra glides should be taken off or left at the ends of the rod; not spaced along the rod. To remove glides, push down on end gate, loosen the cord and slide glides out.

The brackets are adjustable as to their distance from the wall with a set screw. If your rod seems to bend or twist when you pull, check that these set screws are tight and that they are the same distance from the wall.

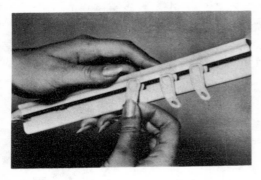

Remove any extra glides to prevent jam.

Install spring type rod without any screws.

Installing and Repairing Shades: Shades are used to keep out light, for privacy and to add to your decor. They can be made of matching fabric, covered with adhesive paper and decoratively edged. Use your decorating talents to make your own. The decorative feature is merely stapled on to a roller, which is the mechanism of a shade. The roller is attached to brackets, one at each end of the window frame. One has an enclosed round hole and one is an open slot. At one end of the roller is a pin end; it fits in the round hole. At the other end is a flat rod; that sits in the slot. The roller must have a proper fit to allow easy roll and take-up. If roller and brackets bind, tap the brackets a little closer to the frame, or even indent the pin holder a little if necessary. If the fit is too loose, take the brackets off and place cardboard shims behind them and re-attach.

If the tension of the shade is too tight, the take-up snaps the shade all the way up. Remove the shade from the brackets and unroll about one-third of the way down. Then hook back into the brackets. Bring up and down several times to re-distribute tension and test. If not corrected the first time, repeat the procedure.

If the tension is too loose, so that it doesn't take up the shade to the desired level, pull the shade about half or two-thirds down. Take it out of the bracket and windup by hand making a tight roll. Replace in the brackets and pull up and down several times. Repeat if necessary.

It helps to spray into the flat end with silicone spray lubricant to keep working parts functioning smoothly.

If the spring is broken you need a new roller, but the shade can still be used. Pry off the shade and staple it to the new roller.

Installing and Repairing Venetian Blinds:
Venetian blinds install into two box-like brackets that sit inside the corners of the frame. Screws come with the brackets. Drill holes and screw brackets in place. The head of the blind slides into the open bracket, and the hinged front of the bracket snaps over it. To prevent trouble, keep mechanism free of dirt and spray with silicone lubricant.

Ladder cross tapes might wear and come loose. They can be resewn. The entire tape can be covered with plastic tape to renew and add color; or it can be replaced. If you intend to replace it, locate the cord knots under the bottom rail. Un-knot them and pull up the cords through the slats to the top. Pry off staples holding the tapes and remove tapes. (If you intend to repaint the slats, now would be a good time while they are all loose. Spray paint is best for this job, placing all slats on flat surface and spraying. When dry turn over and spray other side.) Staple new tape in as old tape was stapled. Insert slats between each cross ladder. Start cord down, alternating right to left between each cross piece until the bottom is reached. Slip through the hole and re-tie the knot. Pull the tilt cord to test slant and tautness of tape. Adjust staples if necessary.

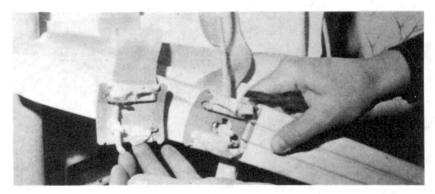

Remove bottom plate to locate knot holding cord of venetian blind.

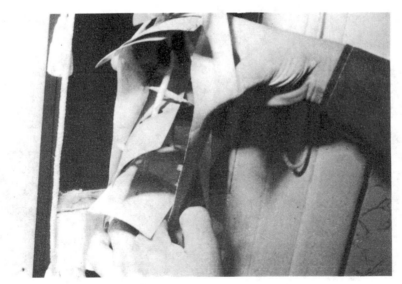

Venetian blind cord must alternate right and left of ladder straps.

The Storage Story

Finding extra space in your home.

Closet Maid

With thoughtful planning, you can double the amount of usable space in your closets.

Today's lifestyle brings an influx of books, records, photo equipment, stereo equipment, trophies and bric-a-brac, creating, for most households, a storage problem. But there may be a lot more storage space in your home that's just waiting to be discovered and used. Look around for new space for shelving. Check the arrangements of your closets. Then use some of the ideas that follow to pack away your goodies in style.

The How and Where of Shelves: Shelves can be put up in the garage or basement on plain L-brackets by securing brackets into the wall (for details, see page 108) and placing one or several shelving boards on top of them. Secure with a screw from the bracket through the board.

Decoratively scrolled L-brackets, put up in the same way, can make their way into the kitchen, bedrooms etc. There are one-, two- and three-tiered shelves made especially for bathrooms that come assembled and just need to be attached to the wall.

Shelves could be constructed from shelving 1x8's which can be butt jointed and nailed, screwed or glued to upright supports, or braced by quarter-round edging. A backing keeps the unit from skewing and wobbling. Masonite hardboard is O.K. for this. Shelves can be constructed to any height, width and length for storage in basement, garage, or laundry room using commercial upright metal brackets and metal shelves, which just bolt together at adjustable levels.

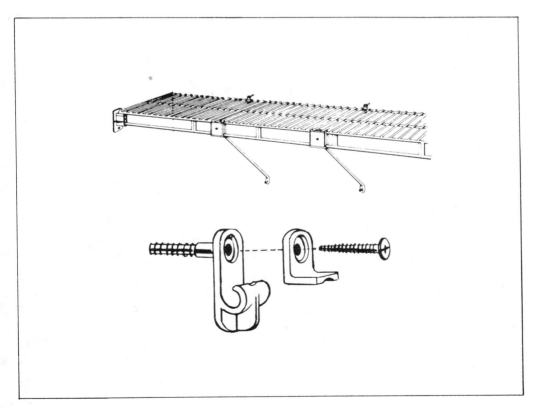

The shelf above is held in the curved bracket by the L-shape piece that is included.

Cantilever Shelves: The easiest, most versatile, most decorative, most widely used shelves today are what are known as cantilever shelves. These have metal uprights, which attach to a wall and have evenly spaced slots from which brackets extend to hold a shelf. These can accommodate multiple lengths and widths, can be variably spaced, and can hold slanted magazine shelves, desk and bar units, or a room divider. They are adaptable to any room, come in many colors, finishes, and styles. They are easily installed or removed and can be utilized for a single small shelf or an entire wall unit.

To install them, determine length and width of area to be covered. Depending on the weight involved, upright standards should be spaced 24 to 36 inches apart, (the more support needed, the closer to-

1. Plan the spacing of standards—the heavier the load, the closer they must be.

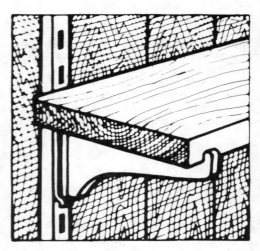

2. Width of shelves depends on what will be stored on them and what look you want.

5. On ¼-inch plywood or hardboard panels, attach to studs or use expansion bolts.

6. To attach on brick or concrete, drill with masonry bit; insert plugs and screws.

108

gether you place them). They come 12 to 72 inches long. Buy the appropriate size and number of uprights. Mark off vertical lines for your uprights and attach with toggles, anchors or mollies. Use screws if you are attaching to studs. Brackets come in 4- to 20-inch widths, to match the shelf width you intend to use. 8 to 10 inches is standard for books, bric-a-brac etc. Decide on appropriate bracket spac-

ing and place into proper slots. Lightly tap in with a hammer for a firm hold. The shelving can sit so that the lip of the bracket holds it in front, or it can extend several inches beyond the bracket. A ¼-inch drilled hole in the underside of the shelf would then hold the tip of the bracket and keep the shelf from sliding.

3. To fasten standards to wood or panel walls, just drill holes and then screw in.

4. For plaster or wallboard, locate stud by tapping, then just screw into the stud.

7. Check with a carpenter's level to be certain that standards are at true vertical.

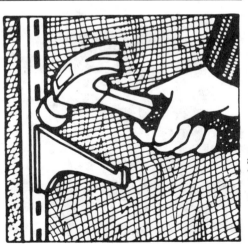

8. Place bracket in standard and tap near the base until it snaps securely in place.

Knape & Vogt

Shelves come pre-finished in assorted widths, lengths, colors, and finishes or you can use unfinished 1-inch thick lumber in desired width (e.g. 1x8) and stain, paint, or cover with adhesive paper to co-ordinate with your wall paper, etc. Just place the shelf on the installed bracket and start stacking.

Additional cupboard space can be made by adding adjustable shelf brackets that just snap into uprights screwed to the wall of the cupboard. Or you can make a pair of 1x2's into a ladder and wedge shelves between the steps. Another great help are the ready-made drawers, which come in several colors and trims and are easily installed with one screw under the cupboard area. They are made in several depths, and are very handy over the counter for storing hand and dish towels, sandwich bags, lunch box cookies, straws, tissue packs, etc.

Other kinds of ready-made drawers install just as easily on tracks for use in under counter areas, where one usually gropes around on hands and knees to find needed items. With these drawers, canned goods, cooking utensils and sundries in the bathroom slide neatly into view.

2. Or drill a hole on bottom of shelf . . .

1. Shelves can rest behind bracket lip.

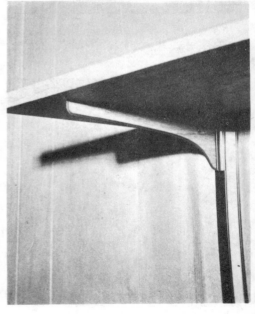

3. And place hole over the bracket lip.

The Storage Story

Creative Closetry: Most homes come with standard shape and size closets which were planned many yesterdays ago around limited and uni-styled wardrobes. With today's trend toward a more extensive and varied wardrobe, closets must be updated to meet our needs and better give the service they were meant to give. The cry of inadequate closet space is mostly a result of inefficient use of closet space. Closets should and can be arrranged to accommodate different sized clothing, out-of-season clothing, and with the advent of today's bulky knits, more foldable clothing.

Most closets are framed 1 to 2 feet down from the ceiling and 1 to 2 feet in from adjacent walls. They are closed by a hinged door or a set of sliding doors, with one clothes pole running across and one shelf above it. This arrangement makes much top and side space unusable or inconvenient.

The ideal situation for space use is one with the entire area accessible and viewable. With today's folding and louvre doors easily mounted on tracks, this is not an impossible dream for those willing to undertake a re-structuring job. If you do not wish to re-structure, you can make numerous adjustments in your current closet set-up.

ADULT   TWO ADULTS

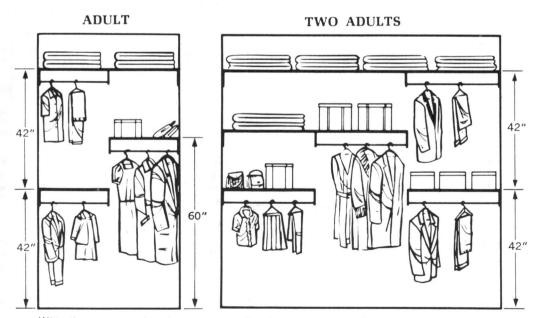

With the proper planning, even a closet as narrow as four feet can serve two adults. Measure your closet, then plan on graph paper where shelves can go.

The Storage Story

If you're willing to do the re-structuring, prepare yourself for the idea of tearing down a wall. It will take a little time, and will make a little mess, but what a knock-out it will be to have a tall, roomy closet instead of the dark, crowded one you've been putting up with.

The framing wall for closets is not built for bearing any structural weight, and can be removed safely and easily. Remove the door (see section on *Doors),* empty the closet, and spread out papers or a plastic sheet to catch the debris. With a hammer and chisel and a prying tool, carefully pry off or chip out the walled area along top and sides. This will expose the framing, which you can then separate at joining points and dismantle. Now your area is completely open. If no stud is located at the corner where your closet wall and your room wall meet, nail one on. Cover and patch with pieces of sheet rock, cut to fit where needed, and patching plaster or dry wall tape. Determine your closet spacing, deciding whether you want one level of doors or two, then go back to section on *Doors* for track installation instructions for folding or sliding doors.

Most ceiling height, therefore closet height, is 8 feet. The widths of closets vary from 30-inches to 5 or 6 feet, and depths run from standard 24 or 30-inch, to walk-in depths. The average width of a hanger is 17 inches, but allow an extra 3 inches clearance for padded garments. Clothes vary in length depending on size of person and kind of clothing. Allowing for hanger hook, rod, and bottom clearance, measure your particular storage needs and your closet space and plan your new closet on a chart.

Consider using multiple shelf rod units, which can easily be installed at any level, plus additional no-rod shelves for boxed and bulky items. Consider too, using the depth of the closet and hanging extension rods which pull out for accessibility. These can also be placed at multiple levels. Closet accessories such as garment bags, hat boxes, and shoe racks are great organizational aids. So go ahead, create a customized closet.

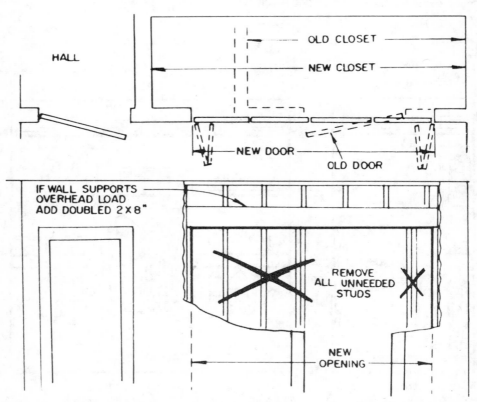

HALL

OLD CLOSET

NEW CLOSET

NEW DOOR

OLD DOOR

IF WALL SUPPORTS OVERHEAD LOAD ADD DOUBLED 2 X 8"

REMOVE ALL UNNEEDED STUDS

NEW OPENING

As a more ambitious project, you can widen the whole closet, or widen just the door.